Beginner's Guide to BEADING ON A LOOM

For my mum and dad, Madeleine,
Genevieve and all who have
supported me.

Beginner's Guide to

BEADING ON A LOOM

Alexandra Kidd

SEARCH PRESS

First published in Great Britain 2005

Search Press Limited
Wellwood, North Farm Road,
Tunbridge Wells, Kent TN2 3DR

Photographs by Charlotte de la Bédoyère,
Search Press Studios

ISBN 1 903975 87 5

Suppliers
If you have difficulty in obtaining any of the materials and equipment mentioned in this book, please visit the Search Press website for details of suppliers: www.searchpress.com

Alternatively, you can write to the Publishers at the address above, for a current list of stockists, including firms which operate a mail-order service.

Publishers' note

All the step-by-step photographs in this book feature the author, Alexandra Kidd, demonstrating beading on a loom. No models have been used.

Manufactured by Universal Graphics, Singapore

Printed in Malaysia by Times offset (M) Sdn Bhd

Conversion formula

Throughout this book bead quantities are given as metric measures (ie: grams). If you prefer to work in ounces, multiply the grams by 0.0352

A special thanks to Liz (TP) for all her handiwork and time. Thanks also to the gang at Search Press for being fab: John, Roz, Juan, Felicity and last but not least, Lotti.

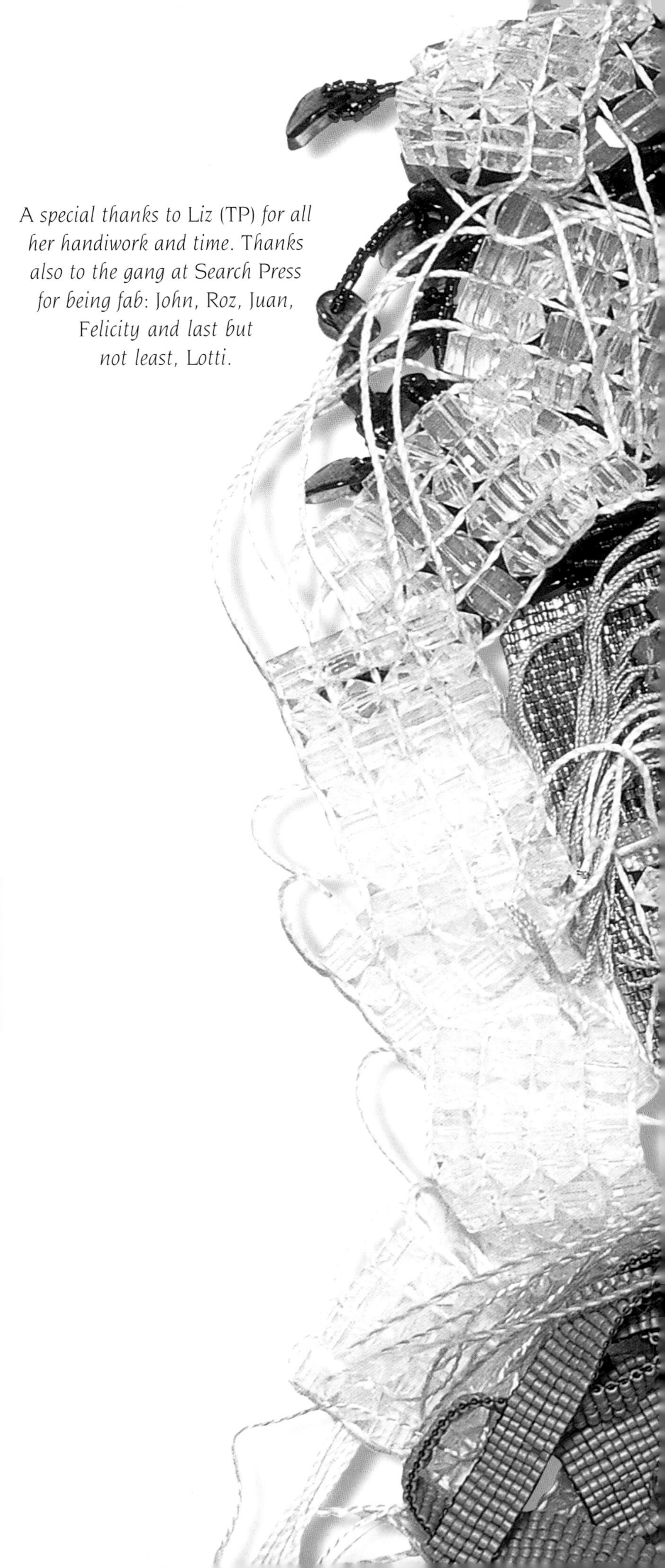

Contents

Introduction

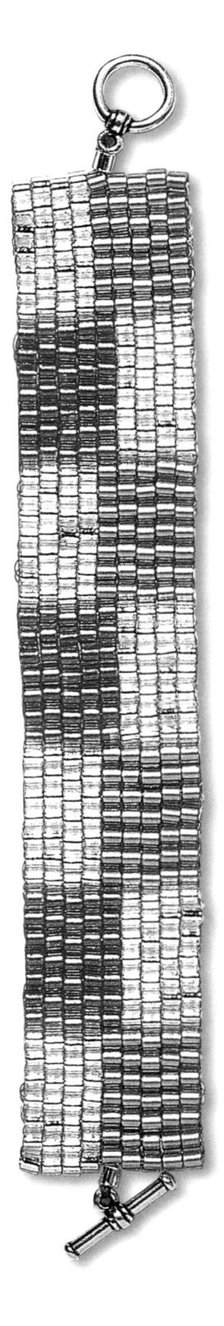

This is not the first time, or the last, that you will hear that beadwork is addictive. Being able to create your own masterpiece from objects as small as beads is incredibly rewarding.

I started beading at the tender age of 15 when my family decided to add a bead department to the craft shop they were running in South Fremantle, Western Australia. The craft bug was already in my blood, inherited from my very talented mum, but once the department was open I quickly became addicted to beading. The beauty of beadwork is its versatility. There are many different styles of beading from threading to hand weaving to beading on a loom. Loomwork is a particularly good introduction to beading for beginners as it is easy to master and gives dramatically beautiful results. You won't need to learn any complicated stitches and you will have the immediate satisfaction of being able to weave a full row of beads at a time.

I have really enjoyed designing the projects for this book and experimenting with different ideas, beads and threads. The basics of beading on a loom are easy to learn, so even complete beginners can soon start to create their own designs. This could be as simple as changing the colours on one of the patterns in this book or using beads of a different size. You will be surprised at how much these small changes alter the look of the piece.

So have fun playing with colours and textures – the possibilities are endless. If an idea doesn't work, you can always take it apart and try again. Be adventurous; some of my best pieces have evolved from mistakes! Have fun doing the projects, experiment and inject a bit of 'you' into your beadwork. Most of all, enjoy it!

Alexandra V Kidd

Materials

There is a whole gorgeous world of beautiful beads and interesting threads out there to discover. I run a bead shop in north London so I am very lucky to have everything to hand but beading materials are readily available in most craft shops and certainly by mail order. You do not need lots of sophisticated or expensive equipment; beads, threads, a loom and a beading needle will get you started. Once you have got the beading bug, there are other bits and pieces that you can add to your kit.

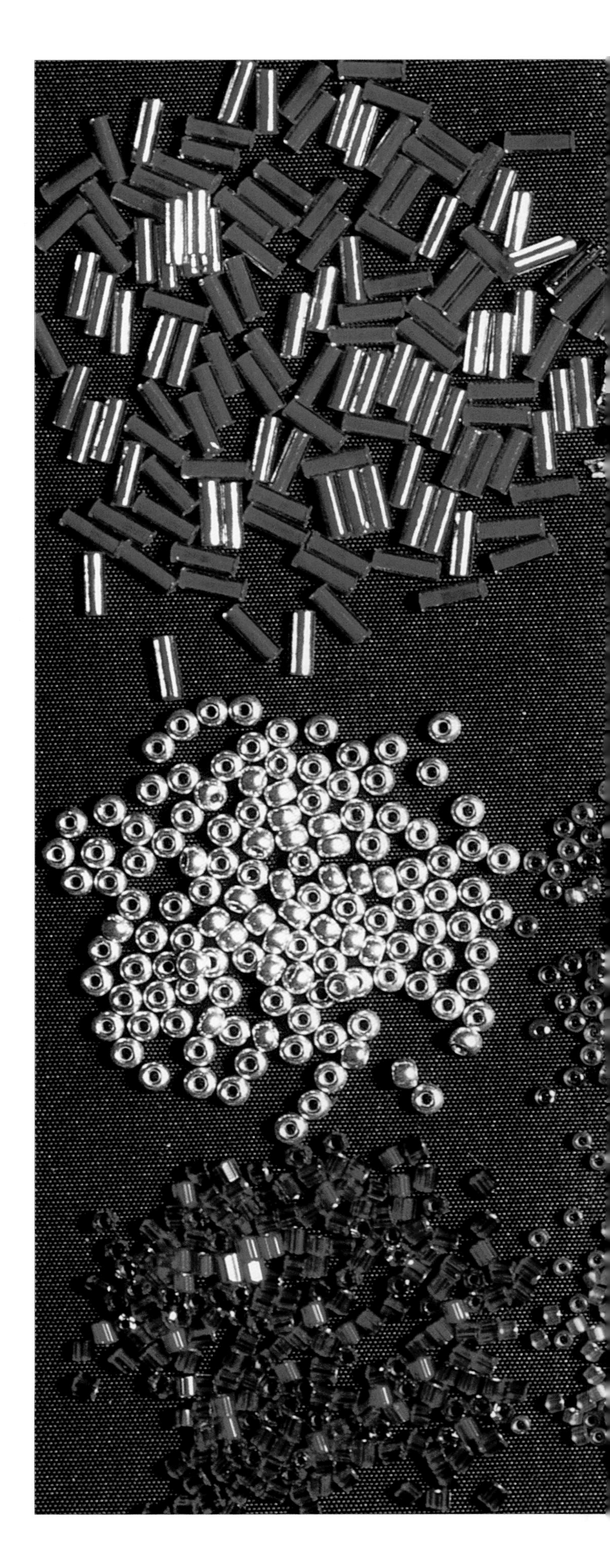

Beads

There are hundreds of thousands of varieties of beads manufactured all around the world. Glass delica beads, seed beads and bugle beads are the types most often used when beading on a loom.

Bugle beads

Bugles are long pieces of glass tubing cut to various lengths. They look fabulous on fringing but can also be used in weaving. Be warned though, they have sharp edges!

Delica beads

Delicas are beautiful to work with, especially on a loom, as they give a superbly even finish. They are widely available in a huge range of delicious colours.

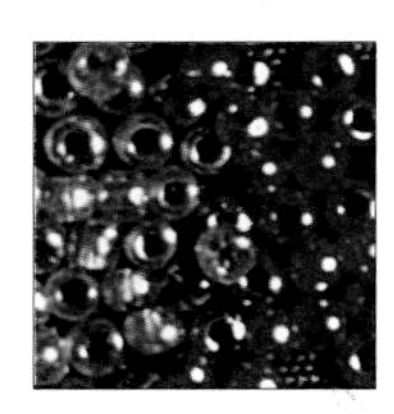

Seed beads

These glass beads are very small and round. They come in hundreds of different colours and many different sizes. The most popular sizes are 11/0 and 8/0. The larger the number, the smaller the bead.

Crystals

Crystal beads are my favourite, I can only blame my mother for giving me good but expensive taste! If you want your fringing to sparkle, Austrian crystals are the beads for you. They are particularly good for bridal or evening accessories and are available in a variety of shapes including bicones, rounds, squashed, cubes and marguerites.

Round faceted

Marguerite

Bicone

Cube

Squashed

Embellishments

Do not be too strict about what a bead is – as far as I am concerned, if it has a hole in it is a bead! Semi-precious stones, pendants, even sequins, can all be perfect for finishing off a piece of beadwork. You can even use feathers if you attach jewellery findings, such as a crimp bead and wire, to them first.

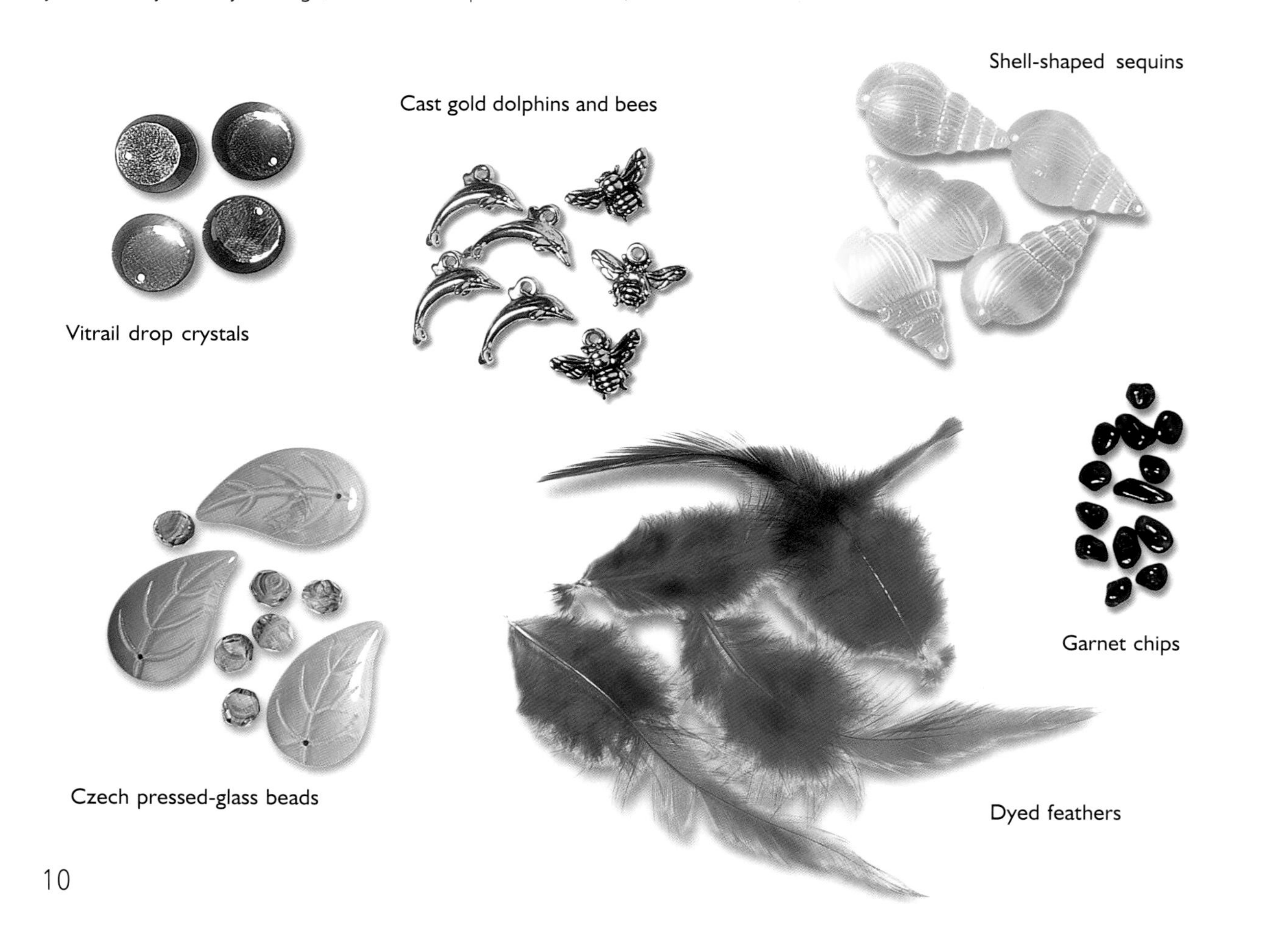

Shell-shaped sequins

Cast gold dolphins and bees

Vitrail drop crystals

Garnet chips

Czech pressed-glass beads

Dyed feathers

Findings

One of the joys of beadwork is that a flat piece of beading can be transformed into a useful or quirky object by adding, say, a purse frame, a clasp or other jewellery findings. When you are making bracelets and necklaces there are many styles of clasp to choose from; the clasps used in this book are but a few. If you are adapting a pattern from its original use, most craft shops can recommend a finding to suit the job in hand.

Clasps

There are many different designs of clasp but the most commonly used are barrel clasps, bolt rings, lobster clasps and toggle clasps. Barrel clasps come in two identical sections that screw together to form, as the name suggests, a barrel. Bolt rings and lobster clasps are the very familiar fastenings used on commercially made necklaces. Bolt rings are round and lobster clasps are teardrop shaped; both have a small jaw that opens and closes. A toggle clasp has two simple parts, a hoop and a bar, but some are very decorative and I use them on special pieces.

Purse frames

A purse frame can add panache to a purse that might otherwise have to be closed with a button. Many different shapes and sizes are available. Most have a silver or gold finish but you could colour them with nail varnish or metal-coating spray paints.

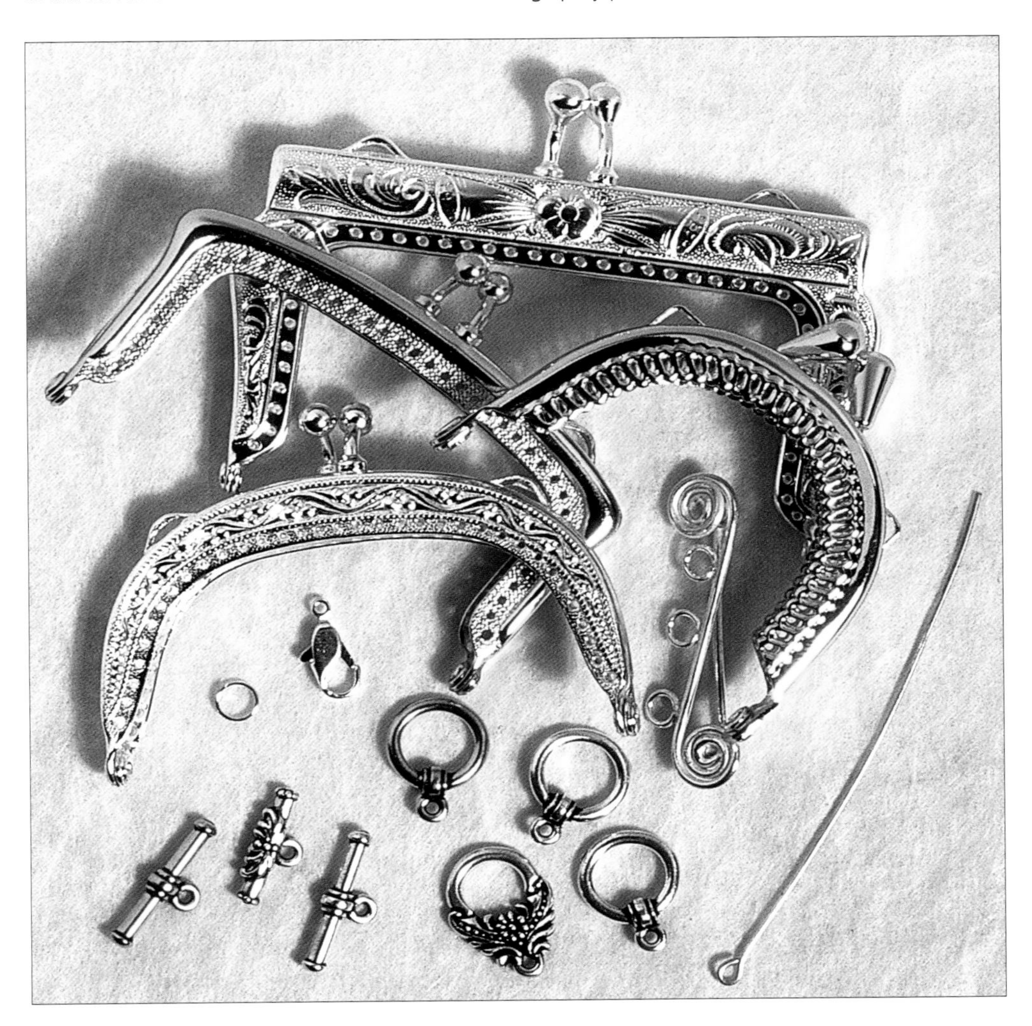

Other jewellery findings

As you get more confident with your beadwork you will find that jewellery findings can be adapted for interesting uses. I used headpins, which are really designed for making earrings, to create draught pieces (see page 57). It is worth investigating the racks of jewellery findings in craft shops to get inspiration!

Needles and threads

All panels of beading have to be supported by warp threads. Typically, the warp threads disappear beneath the beads but they do not have to! The warp is as much a part of your finished piece as the beads you have chosen, so do not miss this opportunity to add a new dimension to your beadwork.

Nymo

Pre-waxed nymo is ideal for beadweaving, freehand or on a loom, because it is flat, almost like dental floss. It is the most commonly used thread for beading. It is a multi-filament thread which makes it strong and means that it rarely becomes tangled. But although it is strong, it is still fine enough to thread through beading needles and small beads. Nymo is available in a range of colours and seems to disappear beneath the beads giving a pleasing finish. I have used size D nymo in all of the projects in the book.

Variegated textured threads

These hand-dyed cotton threads are intended for embroidery but I have discovered that they are fantastic for warping up. They add unusual textures and colours to your beadwork. If you are using large beads with large bore holes, textured threads can also be used as the weft. It is worth experimenting with all kinds of embroidery threads, try ones that are thicker or more textured than usual; it is an education!

Rattail cord

This soft, silky cord is available in 1mm and 2mm thicknesses and many vibrant colours. Rattail cord works well with big beads and it makes a sturdy but attractive warp thread. You can make a chunky piece of beadwork with large beads, or use a number of small beads threaded on nymo between the warps, or even combine big and small beads as I have in the Funky Bag, page 88.

Above
1 Variegated textured thread
2 Leather
3 Rattail cord
4 Reel of leather
5 Nymo bobbins

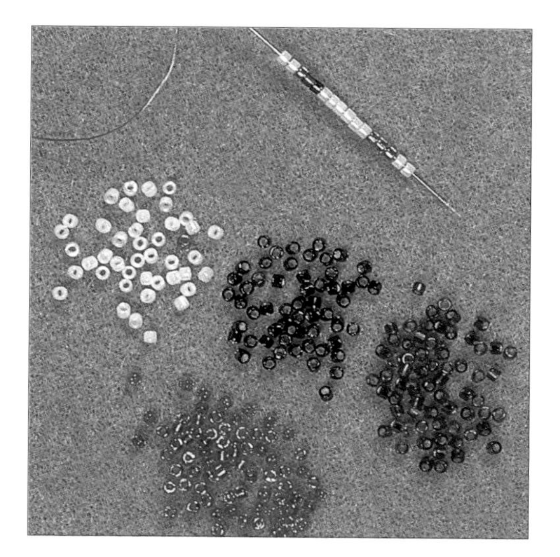

Beading needles

All of the projects in this book were made using a size 12 loom beading needle and a size 10 beading needle. Loom beading needles are much longer than beading needles which means that you can pick up a large number of beads in one go. A beading needle is necessary for weaving loose threads back into the beadwork and for any free-hand work.

Beading mat

It is useful to have some kind of textured surface to put your beads on while you are beading, so that they do not roll about. This can be as simple as a square of felt or a piece of velvet.

Opposite
This green bag was made using rattail cord as the warp. Rows of delicas support each crow bead.

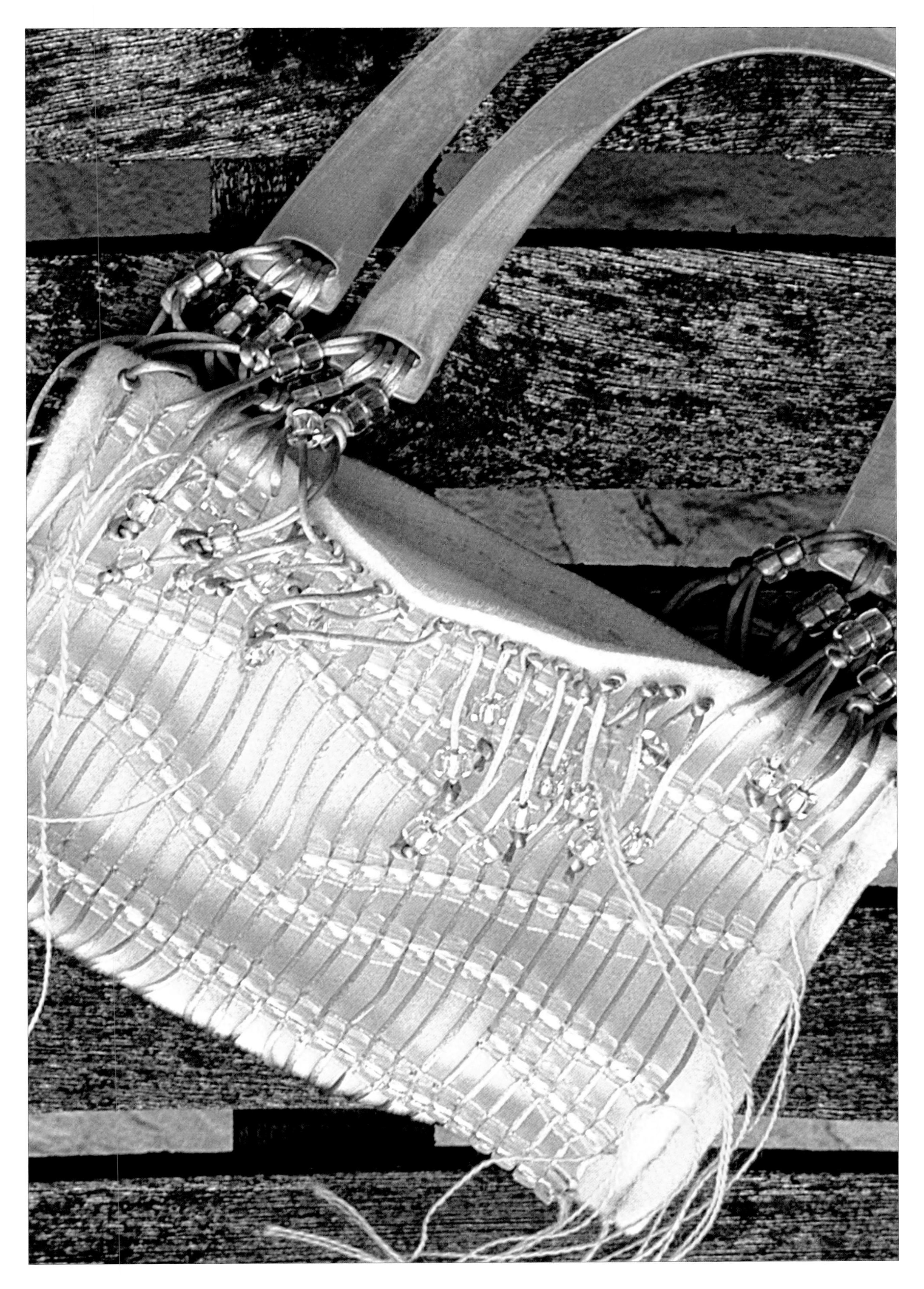

Looms

There are many different looms on the market and they vary in size and cost. The width of your beadwork will be determined by the number of warp threads you can fit across your loom. Most looms come with basic 'getting started' instructions.

Beginner's loom

Half of the projects in this book were beaded on the small, light, wire loom pictured below. This is the perfect loom to learn on because it is inexpensive, compact and has simple screw adjusters at each end that make adjusting the tension easy. It is ideal for bracelets, belts and other small items needing less than 28 warp threads.

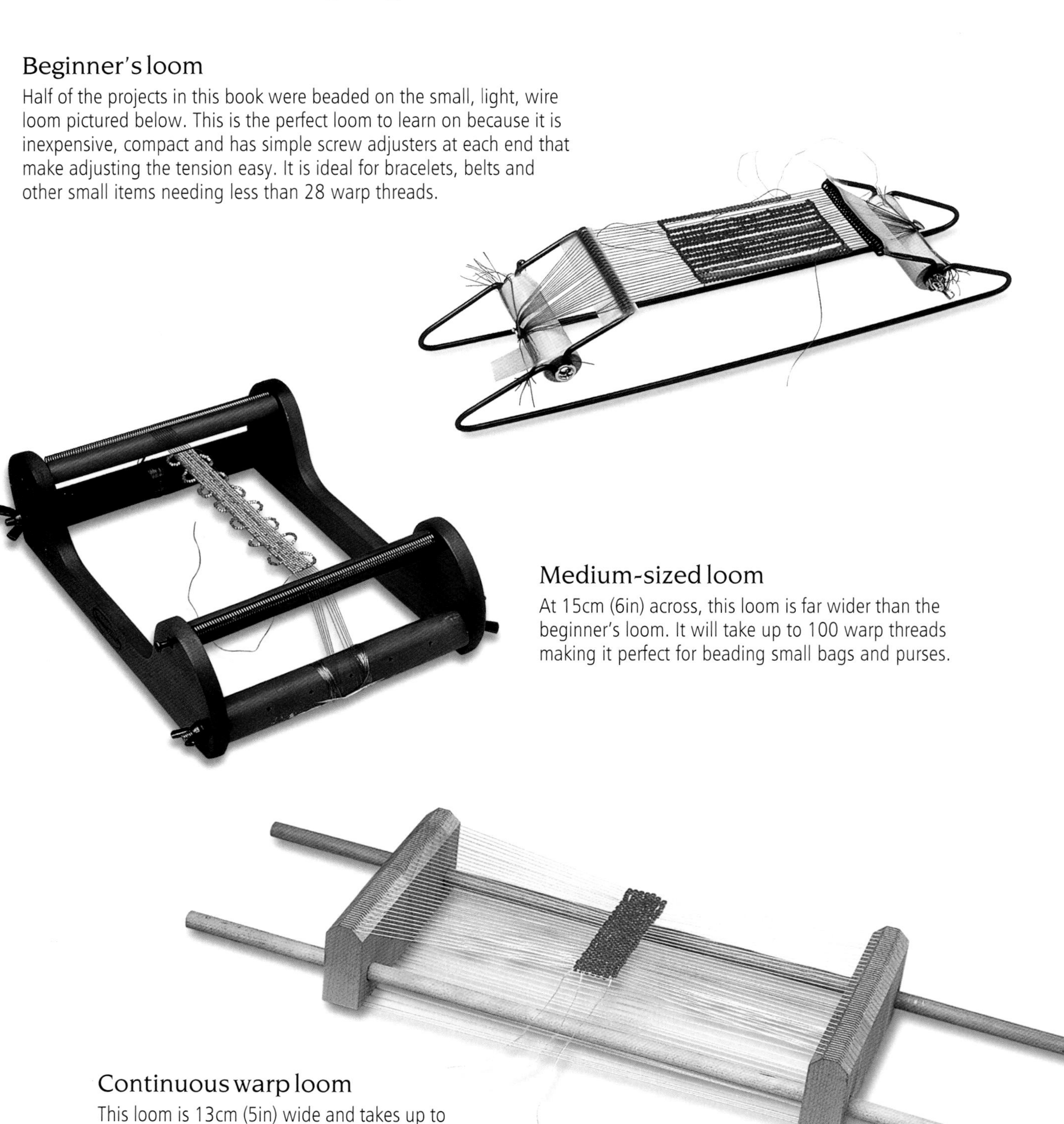

Medium-sized loom

At 15cm (6in) across, this loom is far wider than the beginner's loom. It will take up to 100 warp threads making it perfect for beading small bags and purses.

Continuous warp loom

This loom is 13cm (5in) wide and takes up to 65 warp threads. It is a particularly handy size and you can warp both sides with one continuous thread, doubling your surface area!

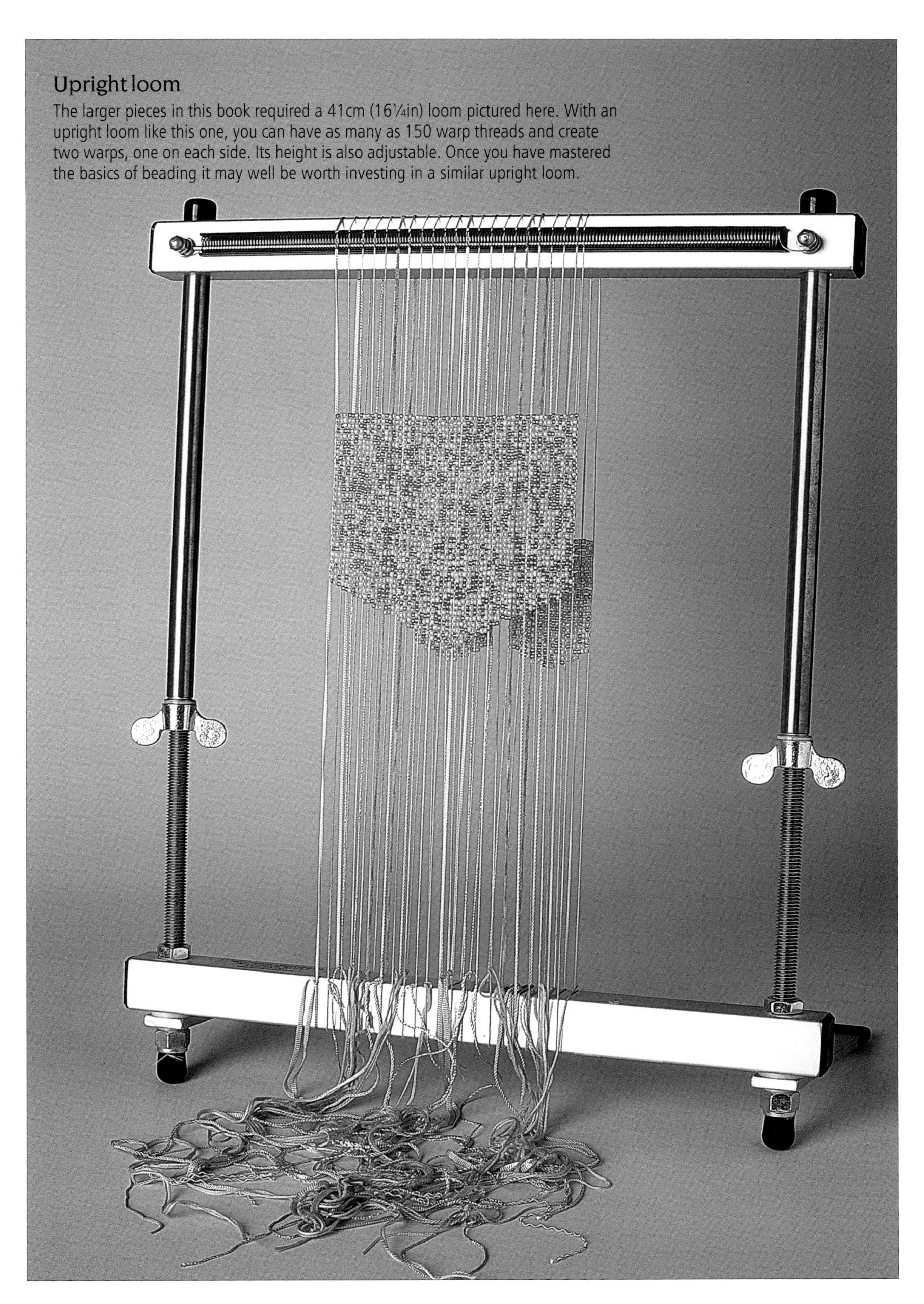

Upright loom

The larger pieces in this book required a 41cm (16¼in) loom pictured here. With an upright loom like this one, you can have as many as 150 warp threads and create two warps, one on each side. Its height is also adjustable. Once you have mastered the basics of beading it may well be worth investing in a similar upright loom.

Other equipment

Beading on a loom does not require lots of equipment but there are a few items that I use regularly.

I use a small pair of **scissors** with a nice, fine end so that I can cut threads without damaging my beading. **Beeswax** can be used to strengthen your thread. Take a length of thread and run it along the wax twice, going in the same direction both times. Be careful not to over wax or it will clog the inside of the beads.

At various times while you are working on a beading project you will find that you have loose threads that need holding in place until you are ready to finish them off. Since you do not have ten hands, make sure you have some **masking tape** or sticky tape close by and use it to hold the warp threads out of the way while you work.

Once you have finished your beading you will need to finish off and perhaps add jewellery findings. **Clear nail polish** secures knots neatly. I find it easier to use than glue because it comes with a nice, small brush. Jewellery findings can often only be attached to beadwork using **strong glue.** Epoxy glue is the most effective glue available and it normally comes as a mix. It is more fiddly to use than other glues but the tough end result justifies the extra effort.

It is worth investing in a pair of smooth-jaw, **flat-nosed pliers** for closing connector rings on jewellery findings and similar small tasks. **Round-nosed pliers** are best for turning loops in wire because they create fewer kinks. Wire cutters are needed to snip through wire and I find that **side-cutters** allow me to get in close to what I am cutting because one jaw is narrower than the other.

Memory wire holds its circular shape, it is fine enough to thread with beads and you can adjust the size of the loop to your own requirements. It is most often used for making necklaces, bracelets and rings but I find it is also ideal for adding handles to small beaded bags. Beaded wall hangings can be attached to any kind of rod but **dowelling** is light, cheap and widely available. Beading is a versatile craft and can be adapted to many uses. You can decorate objects that you might not first associate with beading. For example, in one of the later projects I have added some pazzazz to a plain **bauble.**

I use **graph paper,** a **ruler** and **coloured pencils** to plot out my designs. Allow one square on the grid per bead and then refer to the pattern while you are beading. You will find this far easier than trying to do mental arithmetic as you bead!

Although I have not used **wire** in any of the projects in this book, it is worth a mention. If you want a very solid, stiff panel of beadwork wire is the answer. It is trickier to work with than nymo because it is obviously less supple, but it will give your beadwork a unique quality.

A selection of the tools that I use day in, day out for my designing and beading.

1 Graph paper
2 Nail varnish
3 Wooden dowelling
4 Ruler
5 Coloured pencils
6 Nymo (coloured)
7 Small scissors
8 Strong glue
9 Flat-nosed pliers
10 Masking tape
11 Bauble
12 Memory wire
13 Round-nosed pliers
14 Memory wire cutters
15 Side-cutter

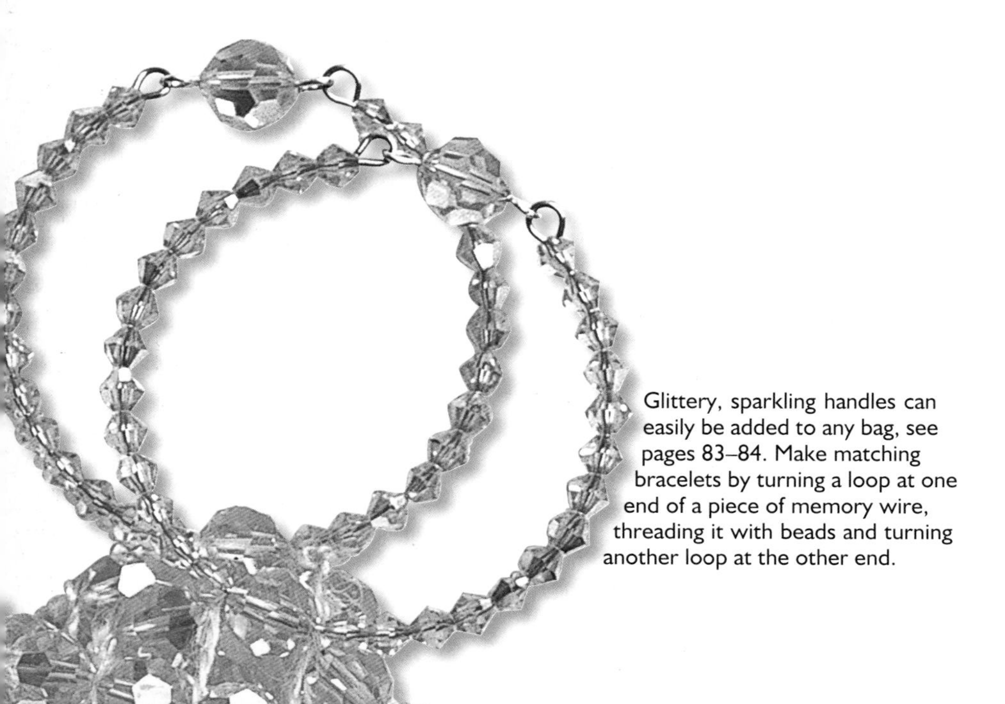

Glittery, sparkling handles can easily be added to any bag, see pages 83–84. Make matching bracelets by turning a loop at one end of a piece of memory wire, threading it with beads and turning another loop at the other end.

Shatter Resistant
1
2
3
4
5
6
7
8
9
10
11
12
13
14
15

Design

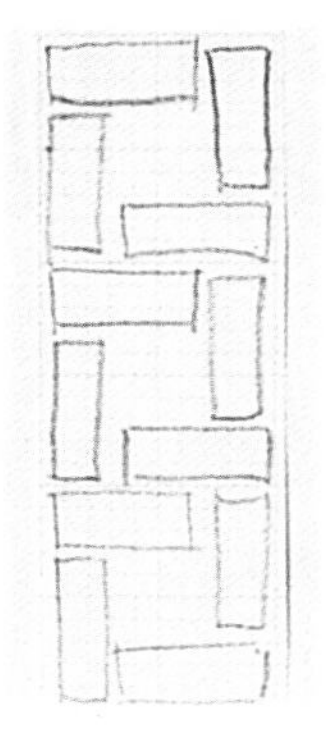

What inspires me to design? Well, I get my inspiration from many different places – it might be a butterfly fluttering in the sky, a sunset, spring flowers or even the print on the fabric of a skirt.

I always carry a notepad with me, and sometimes even graph paper, to get down my ideas. I work up geometric designs on graph paper, shading in squares to make blocks of colour, zigzags or stripes. Using a range of colours, I work in different directions across the paper. You will find that referring to a pattern as you bead is far easier than trying to keep count in your head. Always bear in mind, however, that your graph paper pattern will not match the shape and size of your finished beading exactly. Graph paper squares are perfectly symmetrical but few beads are, so beading ten beads by ten beads will not necessarily result in a square. To work out the true dimensions of a piece, I make a 2.5cm (1in) square block from the beads that I want to use and then count the number of horizontal rows. I can then calculate how many rows, and how many beads, my piece will require.

A graph paper pattern is a great reference point but, as I bead, I may make small adjustments to the design and I might also rethink some of the colours and textures. This is all part of the process. My pieces are rarely made strictly to the original design. So, if you are not happy with your first attempt, do not be afraid to unpick it and try again!

Thread samples, tape measure, early sketches of the kimono on page 79, colour-themed packs of beads and square blocks made from different types of bead.

Opposite
Working from a design

Roman Bracelet

This first project introduces you to the basics of warping up a loom and creating a panel of beadwork. It is the simplest project in the book but you will quickly see remarkable results. Repeat the techniques explained here to complete all the remaining projects. This will be the beginning of your love affair with beading!

You will need

Beginner's loom

Nymo, grey

Beading needle, size 10

Beads:

- Matt grey delica, DDB271 – 5g
- Crystal S/L delica, DDB41 – 7g
- Pink delica, DDB902 – 4g

Scissors

Silver toggle clasp

Masking tape

Clear nail varnish

Crystal

Pink

Matt grey

Size: 2.5 x 15cm (1 x 6in)

The panel is 9 rows by 49 rows.

Use the pattern as you bead and follow the colour key above. Each coloured or patterned square represents a bead.

Warping up

The first stage in any piece of beading on a loom is warping up. Warp threads are evenly spaced across the loom, creating a base on which to weave the beads. Turning the rollers at each end of the loom pulls the warp taut – getting this 'tension' correct will make all the difference to your beading.

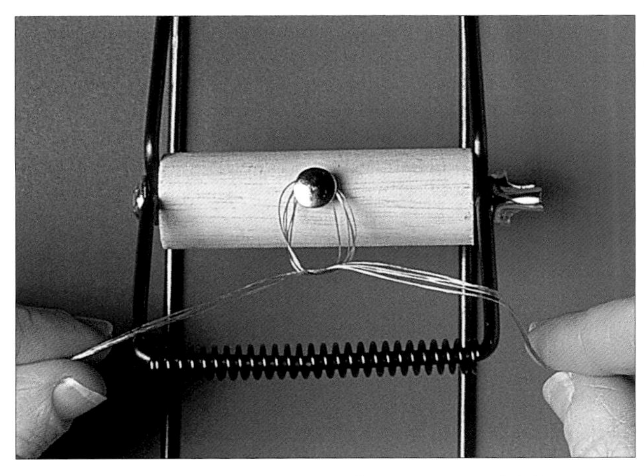

1. Cut five 1m (39½in) lengths of nymo, and fold them in half to find the centre. Now tie the threads around the screw on the top roller. This should give you ten threads of the same length.

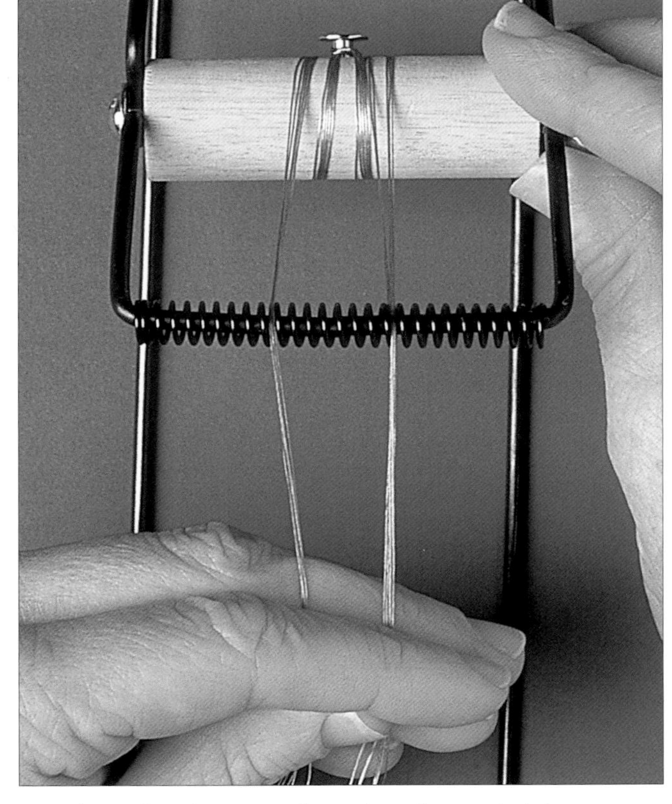

2. Release the wing nut and turn the roller to wind the threads on to the roller.

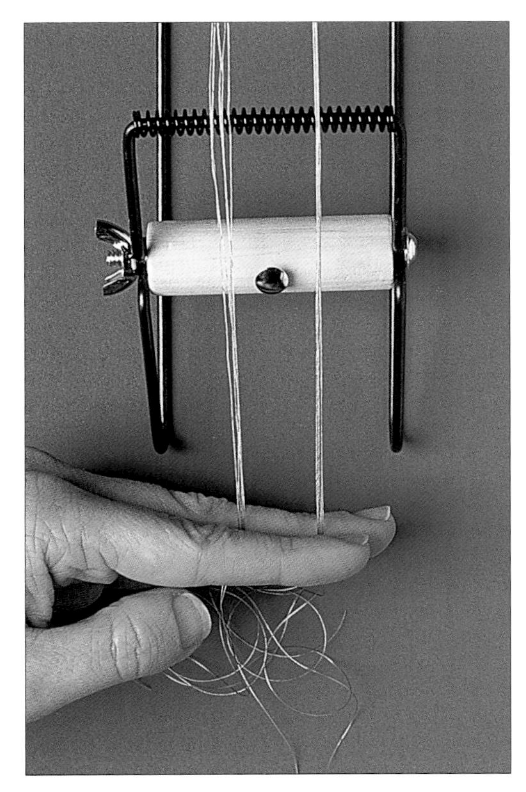

3. Turn the top roller until you have approximately 15cm (6in) of thread left beyond the bottom roller.

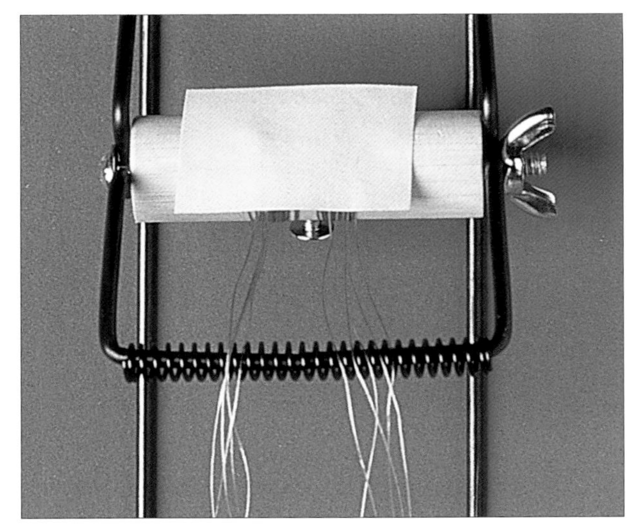

4. Tighten the wing nut on the top roller and secure the warp threads, five on each side of the screw, with a short strip of masking tape.

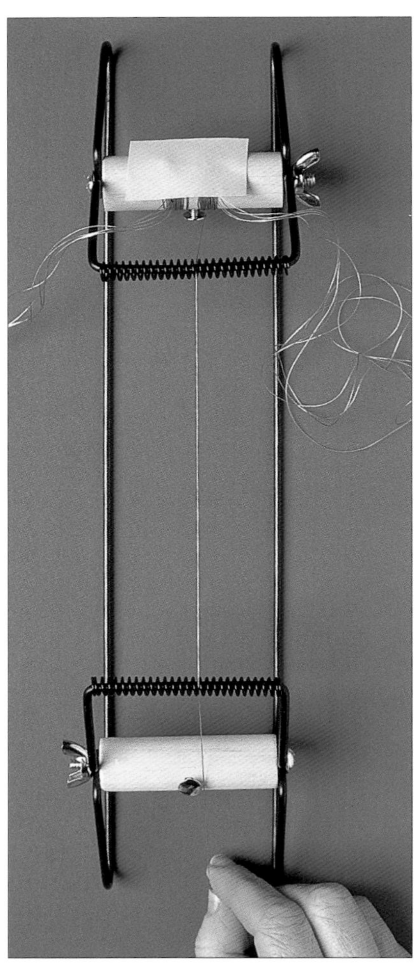

5. Take a thread from the right of the screw. Pull the thread taut and position it between the teeth of the separators at the top and bottom of the loom. Make sure that you have placed it between separators that are opposite each other – you don't want a lopsided warp.

Tip

If you want to use bigger beads on this type of loom, set the threads in every *other* slot in the warp separators.

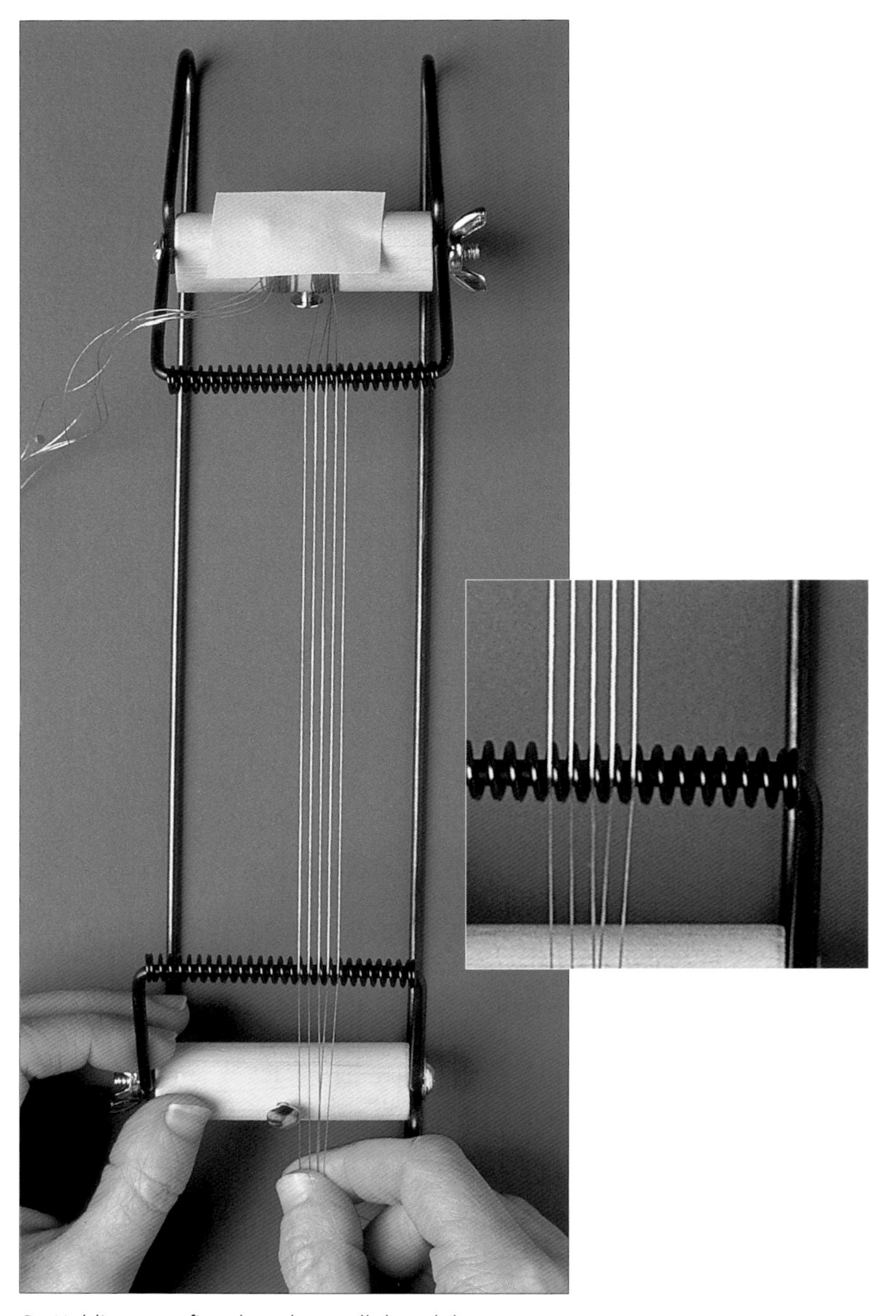

6. Holding your first thread taut all the while, position four more threads, as shown, to build up the warp.

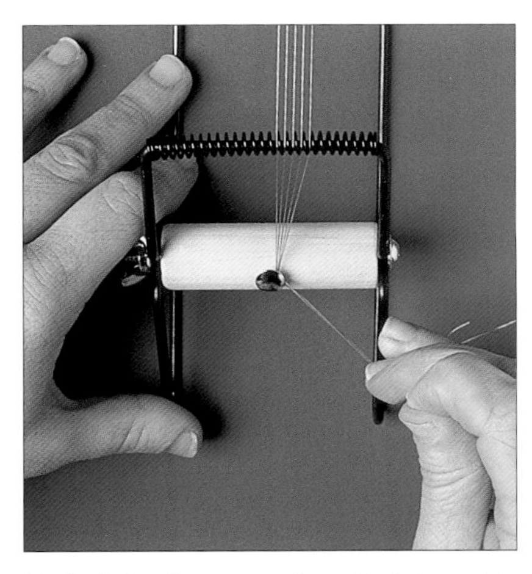

7. Pull the five warp threads tight and wind the loose ends round the screw on the bottom roller several times.

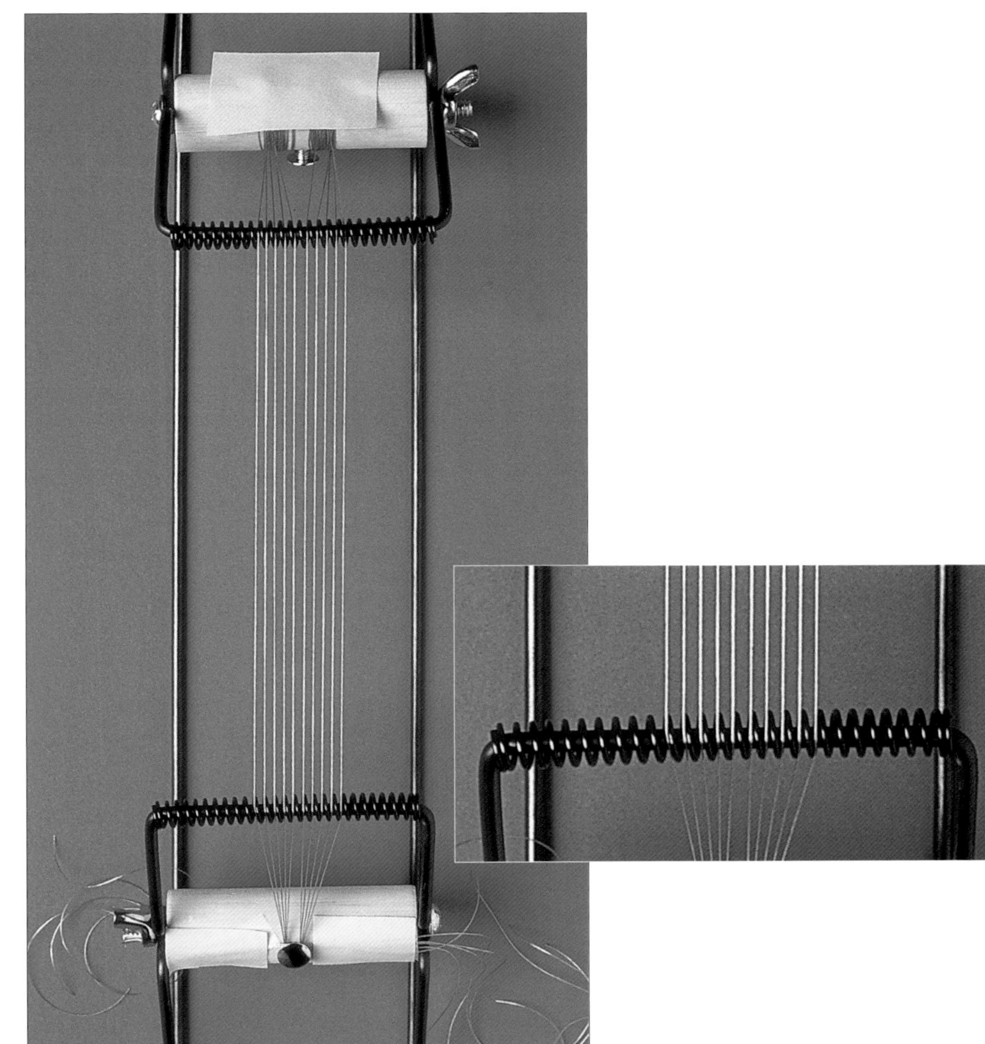

8. Secure the ends of the warp threads with a small strip of masking tape. Repeat steps 5–7 with the other group of five warp threads, working from the centre to the left.

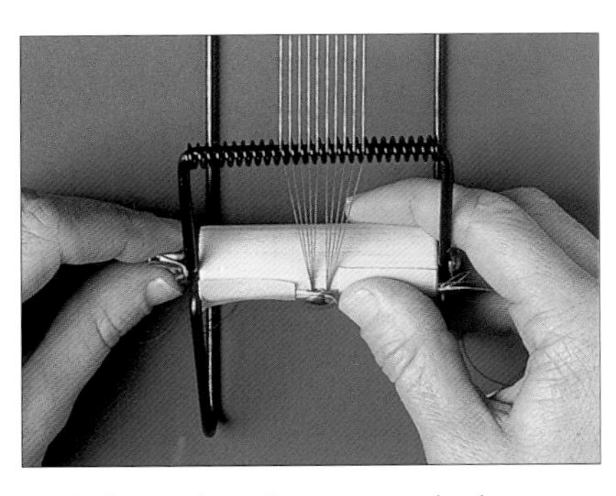

9. Release the wing nut on the bottom roller and rotate the roller to apply more tension to the warp threads. When you are happy with the tension, tighten the wing nut.

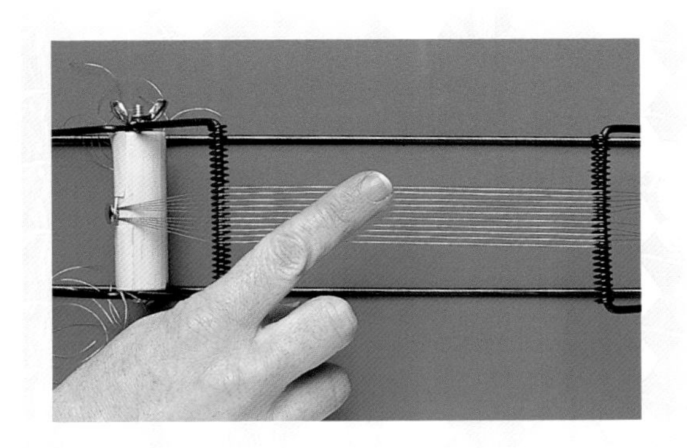

Tip

The warp threads should spring back when you press on them. Adjust the rollers as necessary until you have perfect tension.

Weaving

Weaving beads on to the warp that you have created is a simple and very therapeutic task. Following the steps, weave the weft thread back and forth down the warp, adding a row of beads and taking the needle back through those beads each time. Remember to refer to the pattern each time you pick up more beads.

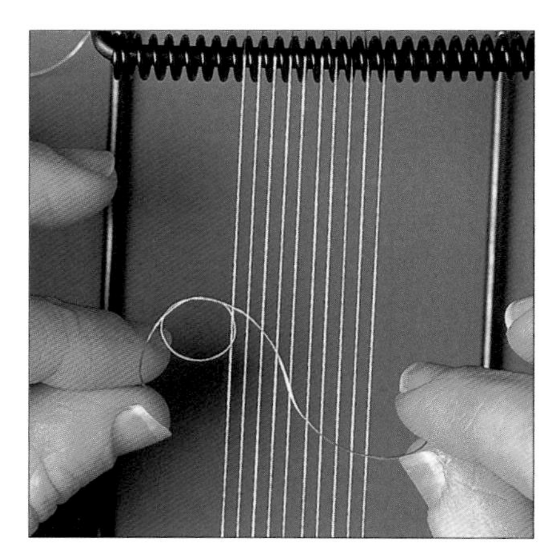

1. Turn the loom round so that the loose threads are at the top. Take a 1m (39½in) length of nymo and use a single overhand knot to tie it to the left-hand warp as shown. This is the start of the weft and it should be placed 4cm (1½in) down from the separator.

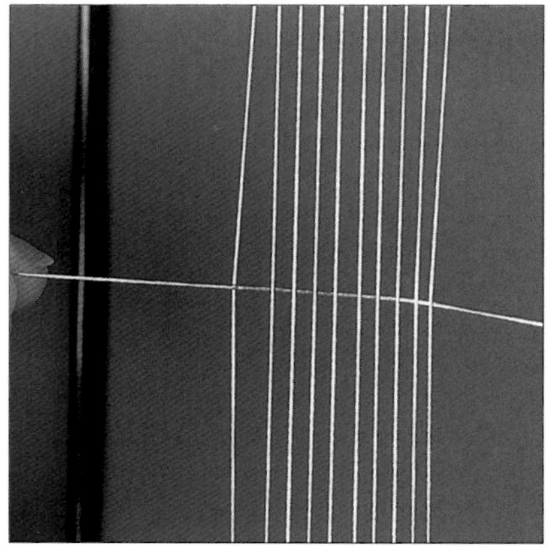

2. Pull the knot tight, then pass the weft thread under all the warp threads.

Tip

Always pick up beads with your needle, never your fingers. Place a small pile of beads on a beading mat or piece of velvet. Then put the tip of the needle in the hole of a bead and use a scooping action to pick it up. Eventually you will be able to pick up more than one bead at a time.

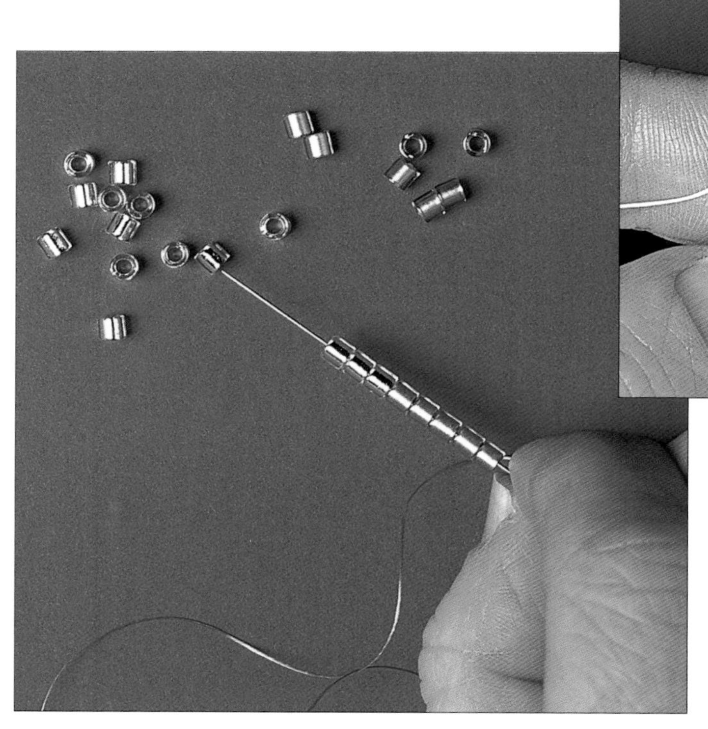

3. Thread a beading needle on the free end of the weft thread, then pick up five matt grey beads and four crystal S/L beads.

4. Position one bead between each pair of warp threads. The beads will make the width of the warp increase slightly because they are bigger than the spaces between the threads.

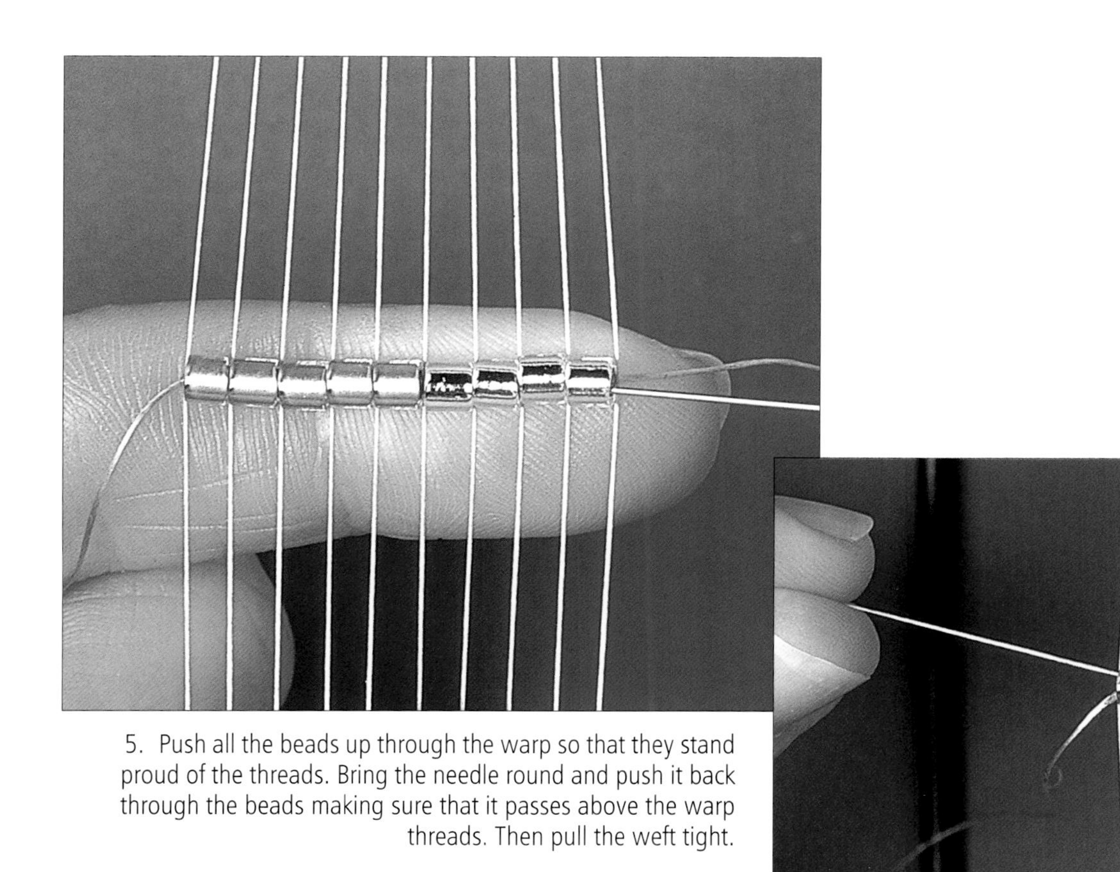

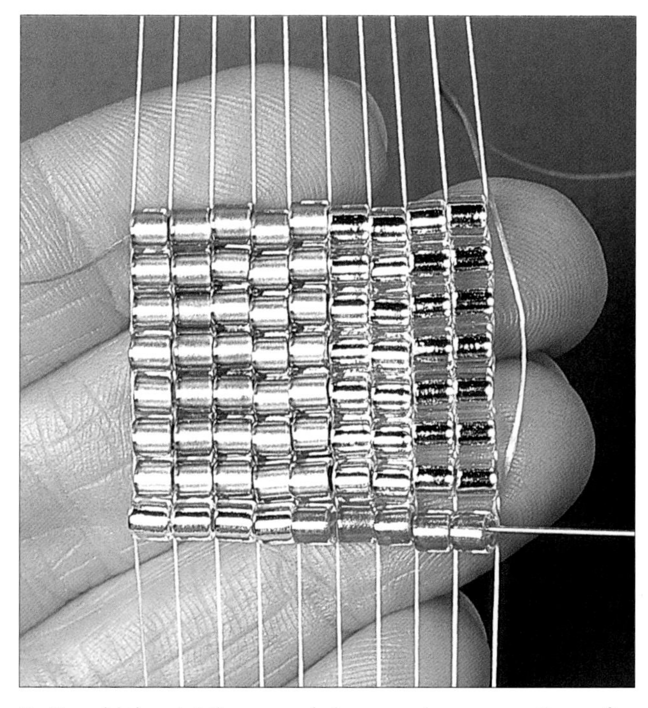

5. Push all the beads up through the warp so that they stand proud of the threads. Bring the needle round and push it back through the beads making sure that it passes above the warp threads. Then pull the weft tight.

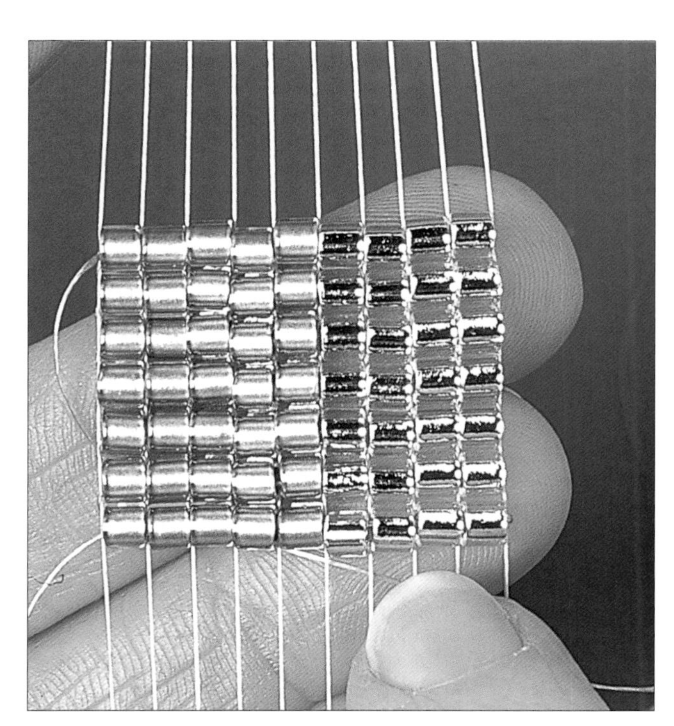

6. Pass the weft thread back under the warp back to the right-hand side, reload the needle with beads and repeat steps 4–5 until you have seven rows of matt grey and crystal S/L beads. Adjust the beads as you work, making sure that the lines are straight and square to the warp.

7. To add the eighth row and change colours, pass the weft thread under the warp to the right-hand side and pick up four crystal S/L and five pink beads. Repeat steps 4–5 to weave them on to the warp.

Joining weft threads

At some stage you will run out of weft thread. Thankfully, adding a new thread is simple as the following steps demonstrate. Each new thread should be roughly 1 m (39½in) which is long enough to work with, but not so long that the thread might tangle.

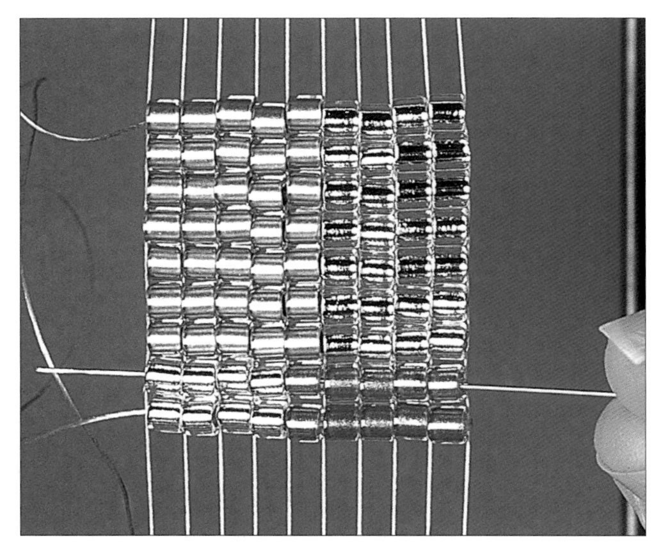

1. When you have approximately 20cm (7¾in) of weft thread left, feed the needle back through the second row up from the bottom, left to right.

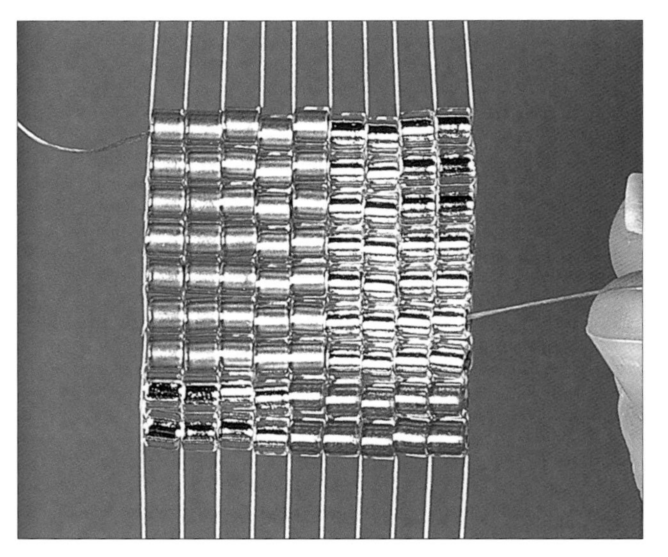

2. Now feed it right to left through the third row up and left to right through the fourth row up.

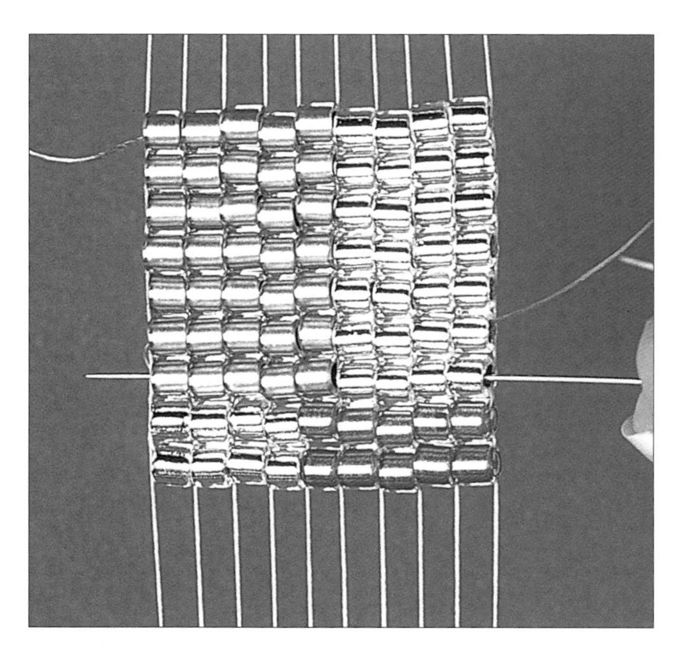

3. Re-thread your needle with a new length of thread and pass the new weft thread from right to left, through the beads in the third row. Do not pull the thread all the way through, leave some excess at the end.

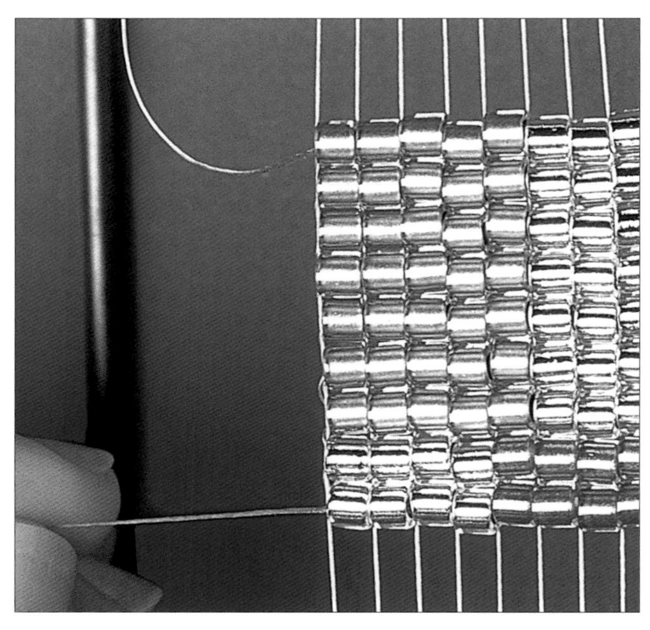

4. Weave the new weft thread from left to right through the second row from the bottom and then right to left through the bottom row. Now continue to add rows of beads with the thread on the left-hand side, following the pattern on page 20.

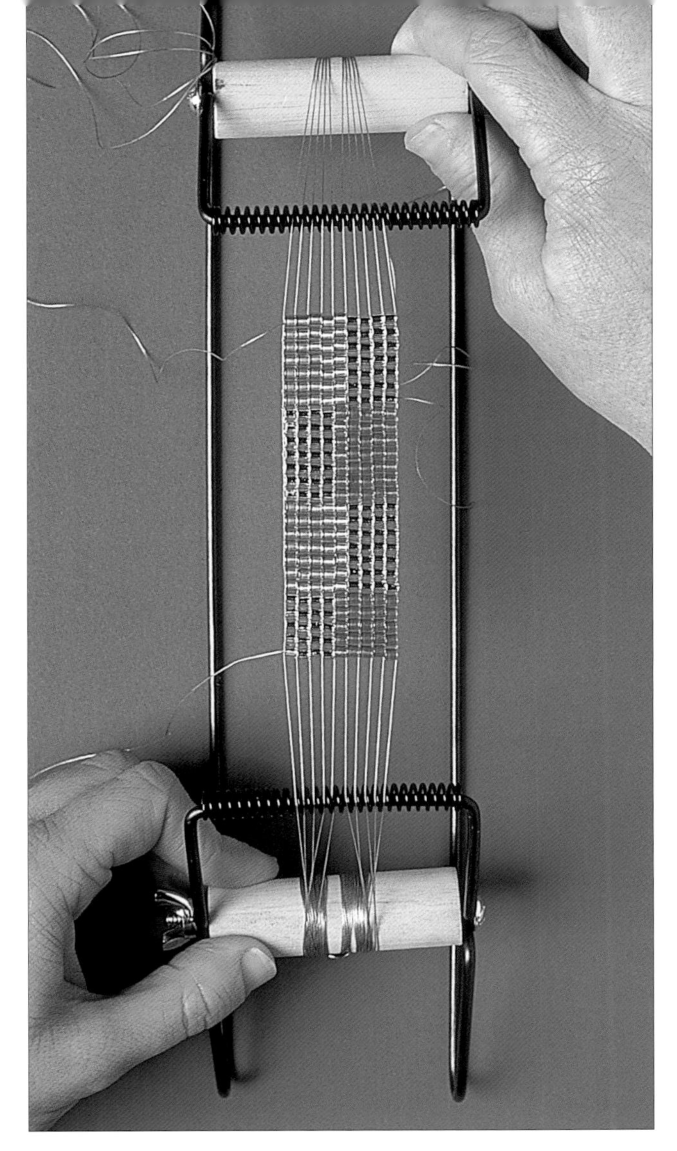

5. As the beadwork nears the bottom of the loom, you must move the beading up the loom so that you can continue to add rows. To wind on, remove the masking tape, release both wingnuts and carefully turn both rollers together.

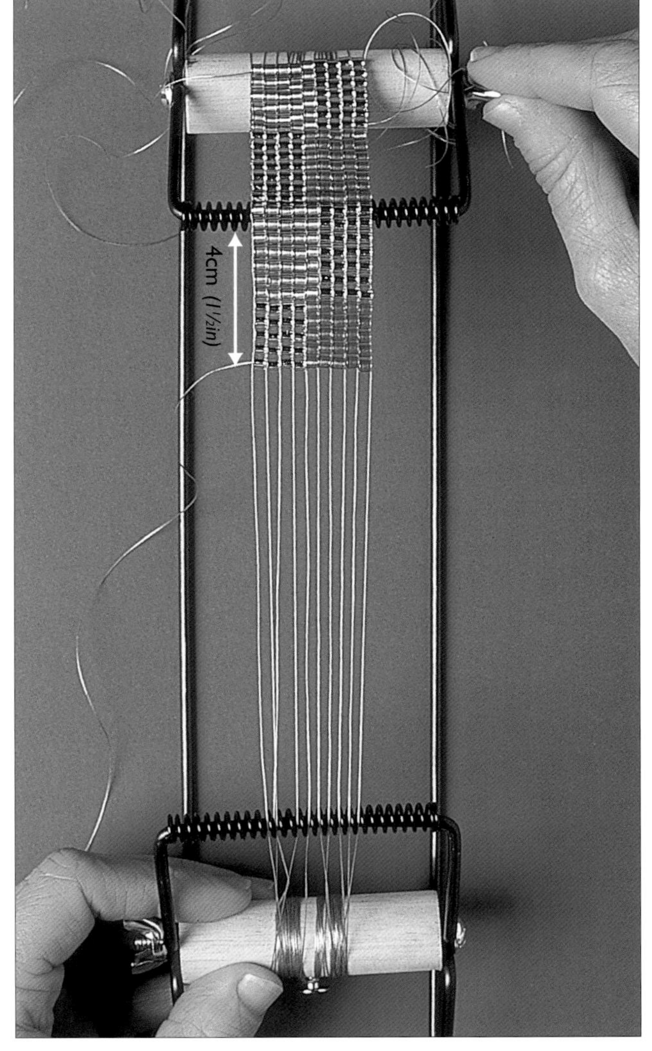

6. Keep turning the rollers until the bottom row of beads is approximately 4cm (1½in) below the top warp separators, then tighten the wing nuts.

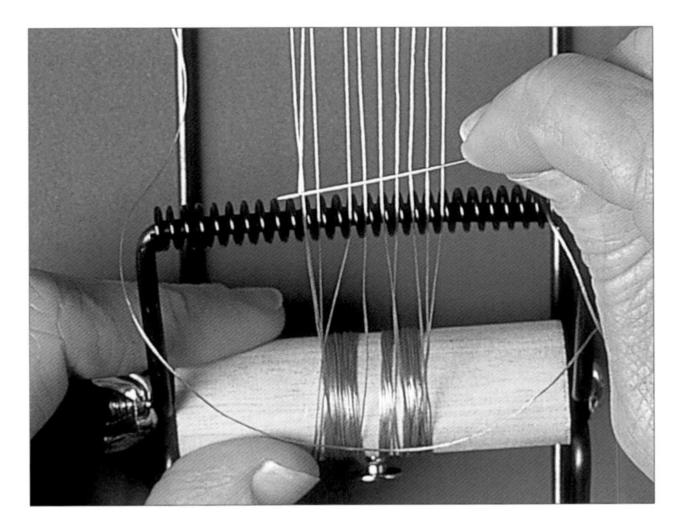

7. When winding on, the warp threads sometimes come out of the separators. Reposition them with the needle.

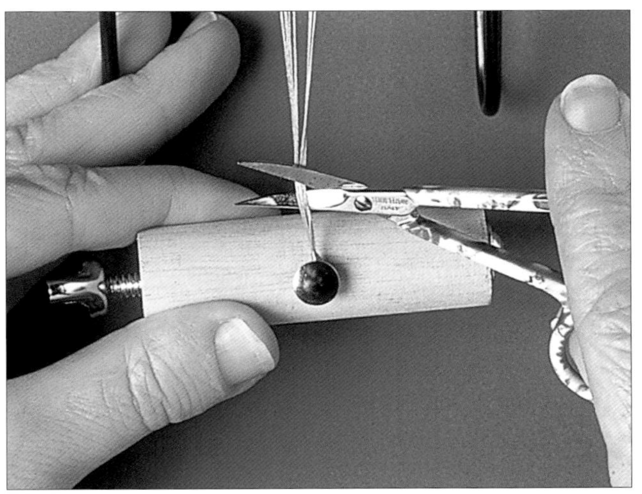

8. When you have beaded the whole design, release the bottom roller and unwind the warp threads. Cut them off next to the screw. Then snip off any excess threads along the sides of the beading. Snip close to the beading and the nymo will spring back and disappear inside the beads.

Finishing off

Once the weaving is complete, you need to patiently end off each warp thread in order to hold the beading together.

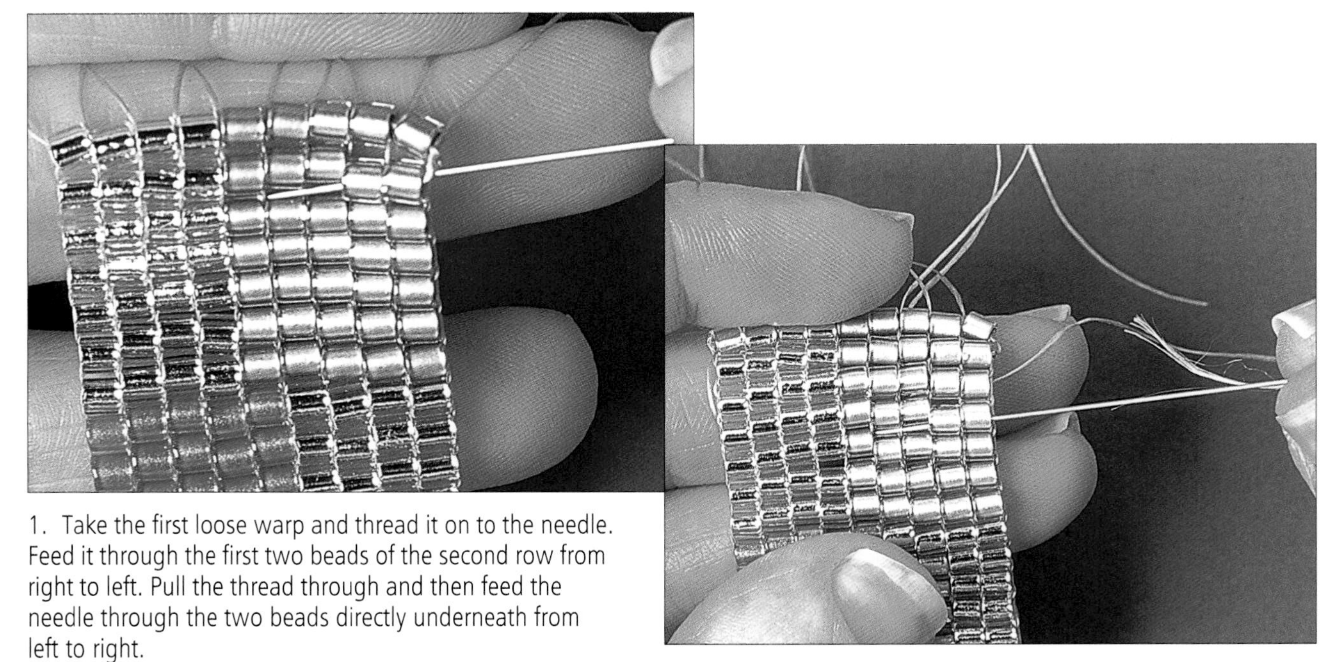

1. Take the first loose warp and thread it on to the needle. Feed it through the first two beads of the second row from right to left. Pull the thread through and then feed the needle through the two beads directly underneath from left to right.

2. Now bring the needle from right to left through the first two beads of the fourth row down. Pull the thread tight and snip off the excess close to the beading.

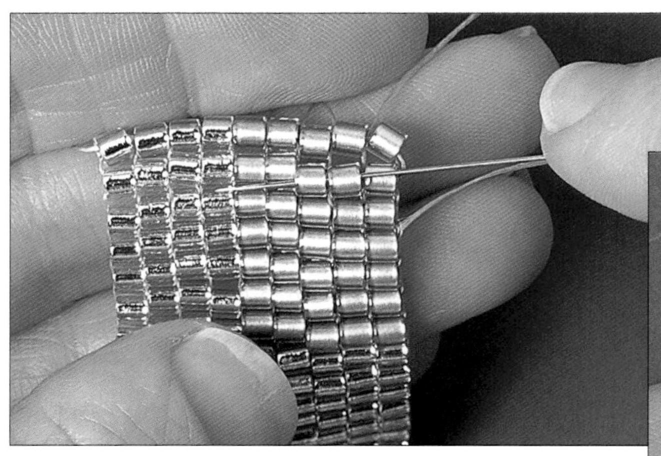

3. Now thread the second loose warp on to the needle. Weave it back and forth down the beading as before but this time weave through the beads in the second and third vertical rows.

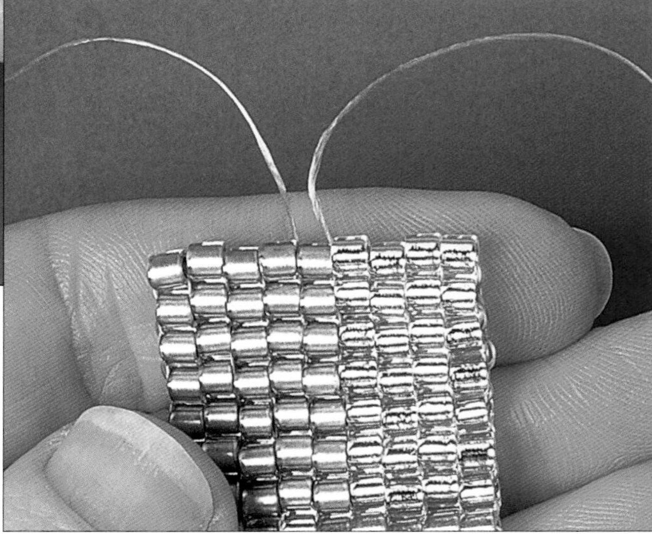

4. Finish off each warp thread except the two in the middle. Turn the beading round and finish off the other end in the same way, leaving two loose threads in the middle.

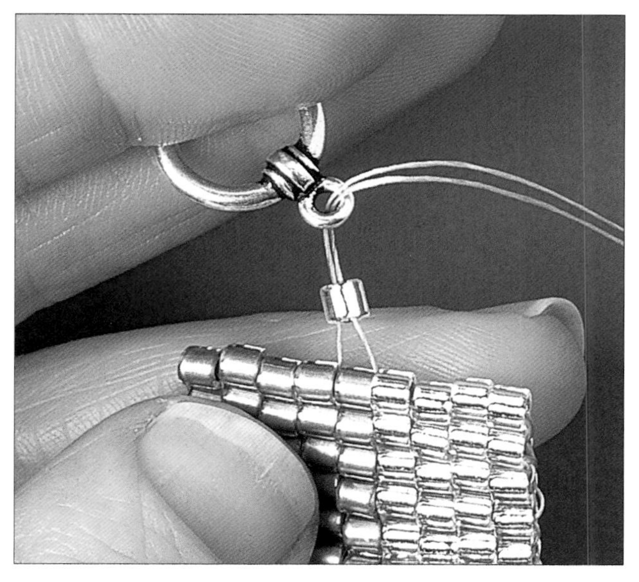

5. Thread the two remaining warp threads at one end of the bracelet on the needle. Pick up one crystal S/L bead then pass the needle through the connector ring of the clasp.

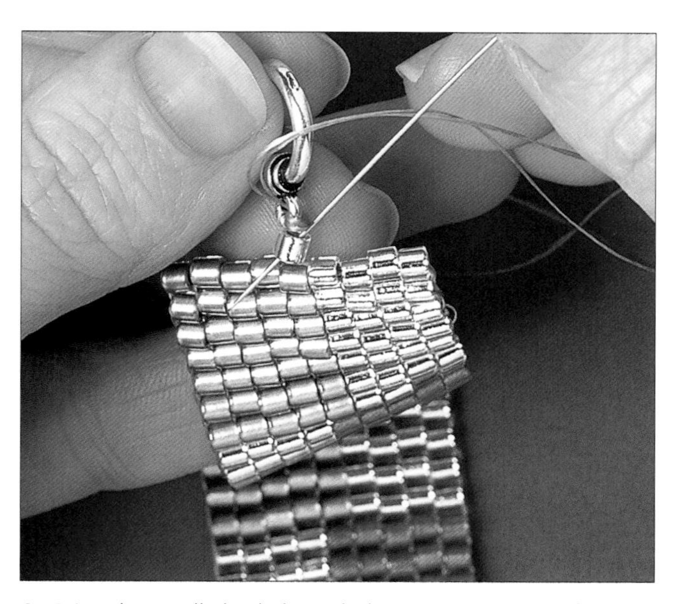

6. Bring the needle back through the connector ring to form a slack loop. Pass the needle through the loop and then through the bead. Carefully pull the thread to bring the connector ring and bead together. Pull the knot tight, pass the needle back through the ring, knot again and take the threads down through the bead.

7. Finally, weave the warp ends down through four rows of the bracelet as before and trim off the excess threads.

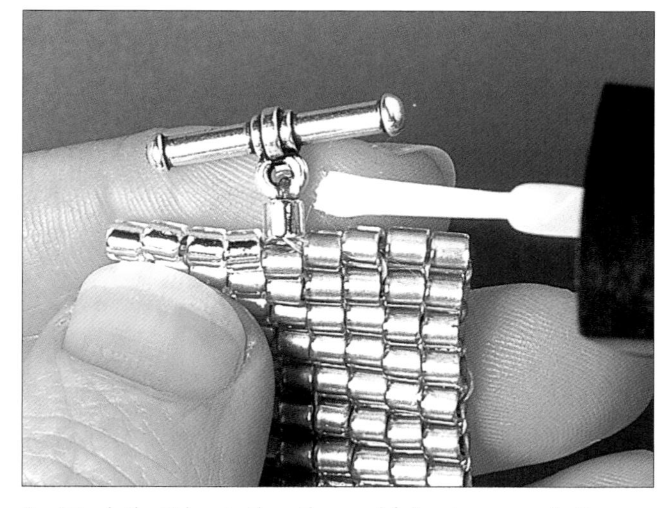

8. Attach the T-bar to the other end following steps 5–7. Apply a spot of clear nail varnish to the threads on the connector ring on the hoop and on the T-bar.

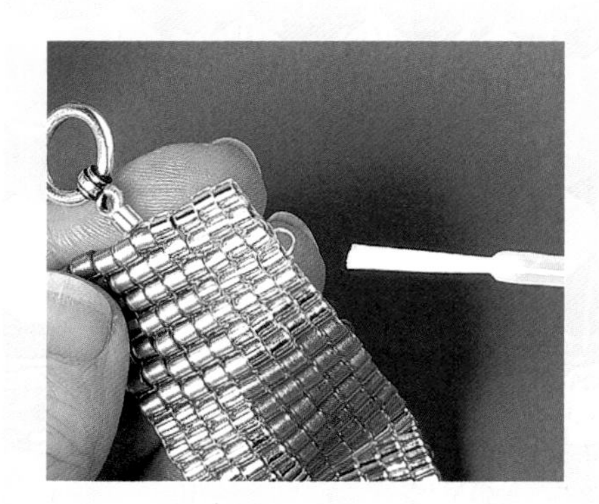

Tip

When weaving in warp ends you often get 'loose' loops along the edge of the beadwork. You can use clear nail varnish to 'glue' down these loose loops. Dab the varnish on the thread with the brush then press the thread flat with your finger.

Opposite
The gleaming, silver-lined beads next to matt grey ones creates a great texture combination and the pink beads add some soft, sultry colour.

This one-colour bracelet is fun and chunky. It is good to practise with reasonably big beads like these while you are learning to bead on a loom.

Braided Belt

When you first start beading it is easy to be so entranced by the beads that you overlook the warp, but beautiful threads are not just for embroidery! This belt has blocks of beading spaced out along some gorgeous warp threads which are knotted at each end. It is simple and stylish. If you want to make the belt a specific length remember to allow at least 30cm (11¾in) extra thread at each end for the ties.

You will need

Beginner's loom

14 variegated textured threads, 140cm (55¾in)

Nymo, olive green

Beading needle, size 10

Beads:

- Seed LBC605, size 8/0
- Dark green iris – 45g

Scissors

Masking tape

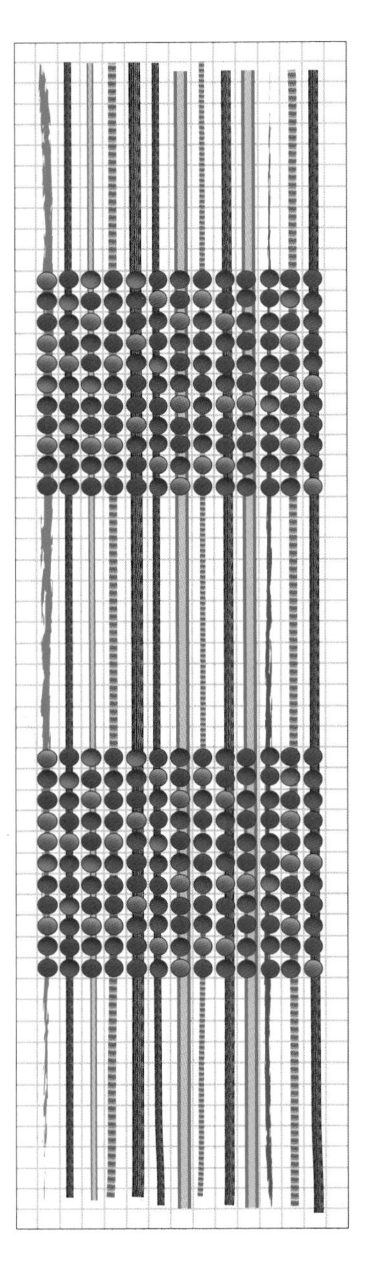

Each coloured circle on the pattern represents a bead.

Size: 133 x 3cm (53 x 1¼in)

Each block has 11 rows of 13 beads. There are ten blocks in total.

1. Cut fourteen warp threads to length, tie a knot 30cm (11¾in) from one end and anchor this to one of the rollers on the loom. Wind the warp threads on to the roller, space the threads across the warp separators and secure the loose ends to the other roller on the loom with masking tape. With this type of warp thread, you will find it best to stick a strip of masking tape across the warp separators.

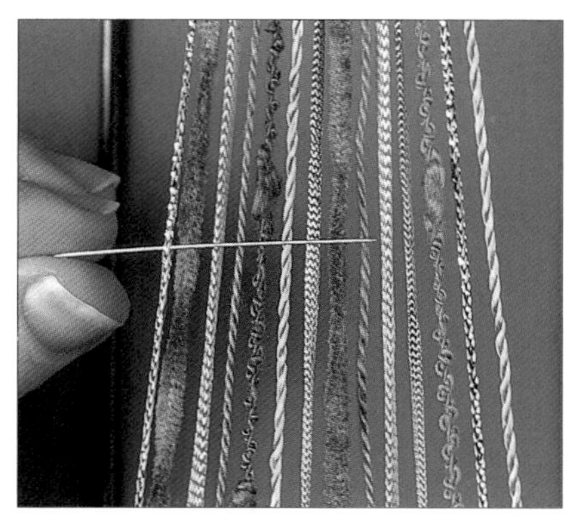

2. Bring both ends of a 2m (79¼in) length of nymo together and thread them both on to the needle. Take the doubled thread through the centre of the left-hand warp thread.

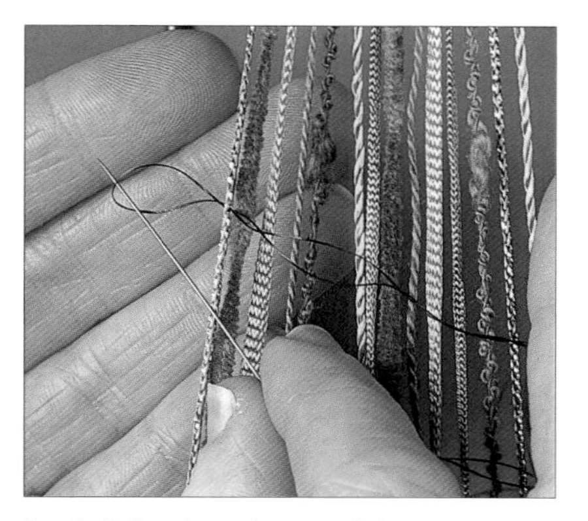

3. Pull the thread most of the way through but leave the loop at the end. Now bring the needle round through the loop and pull the thread to tighten the knot.

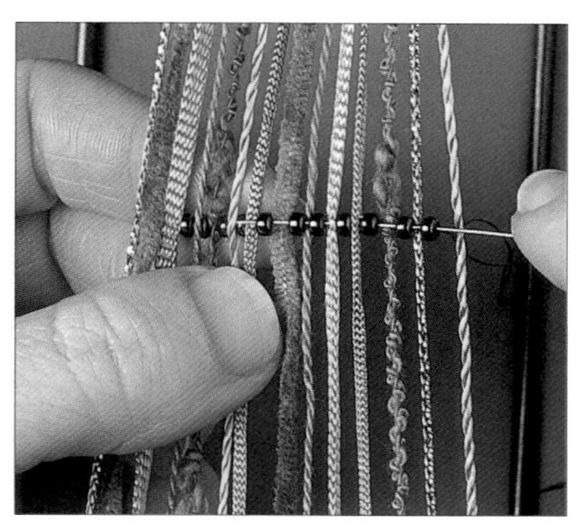

4. Now that the weft thread is knotted to the warp, take the weft under the warp and out on the right-hand side. Pick up thirteen beads, set them between the warp threads and pass the needle back through all beads. Do not worry if you catch any warp threads.

5. Work eleven rows of thirteen beads to make each beaded block on the belt. Space the blocks approximately 3.5cm (1⅜in) apart.

6. When you have beaded all the blocks, remove the beadwork from the loom and knot pairs of warp threads together at both ends.

7. Slide your fingers up the threads to tighten the knot close to the beadwork.

8. Gather all the warp threads at one end of the belt together and tie an overhand knot with them all. Repeat at the other end.

Variegated textured threads create a beautiful wave of colour that contrasts with the dark, shiny beads.

White opal bicones and cubes woven on to a white warp make a glamorous belt. You could loop this piece of beading around your neck and wear it as a unique and stylish necklace.

Moonlight Purse

It is incredibly easy to turn a flat piece of beading into a useful and beautiful object. Here a beaded panel is transformed into an elegant evening purse by simply folding it in half and adding a purse frame.

You will need

Continuous warp loom

Nymo, grey

Loom beading needle, size 12

Beading needle, size 10

Beads, delica:

- Green, DB168 – 1.5g
- Burgundy, DB296 – 2.5g
- Mauve, DB146 – 2g
- Yellow, DB145 – 1g
- Silver, DB38 – 45g

Scissors

Silver purse frame, hinged, 7cm (3in) wide

Green

Burgundy

Yellow

Mauve

Silver

Overall size: 7.5 x 18cm (3 x 7in)

The panel has 178 rows of 48 beads and measures 30cm (11¾in) from top to bottom.

In this pattern, every square represents a bead. Follow the colour key as you work. The pattern shows the front and back of the purse but the panel should be beaded as one continuous panel, as shown on page 37.

Front

Back

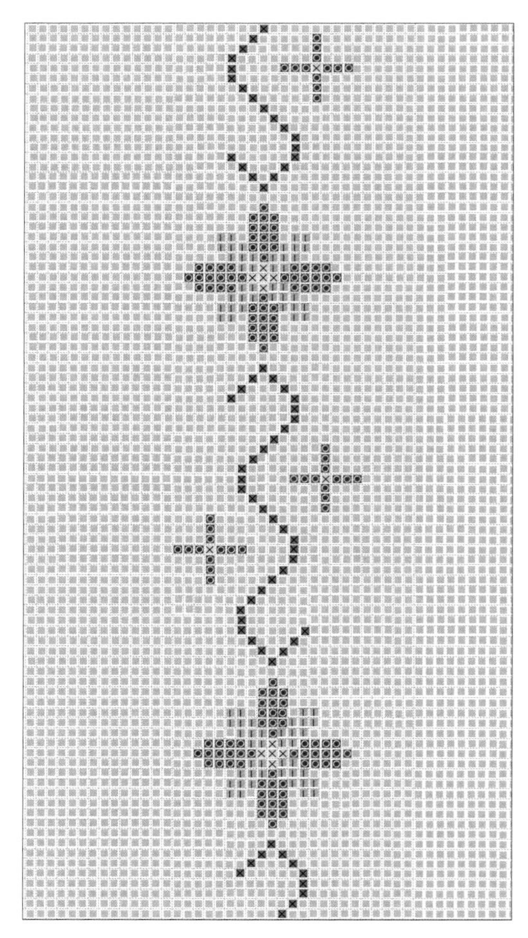

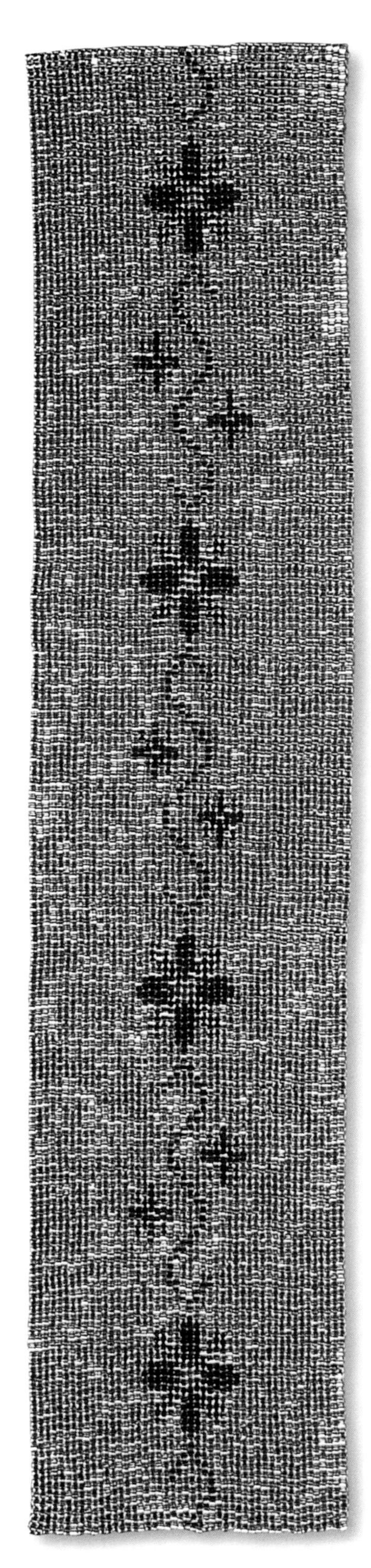

1. Warp your loom with 49 threads and weave the pattern on the opposite page. Cut it off the loom and finish off all the threads.

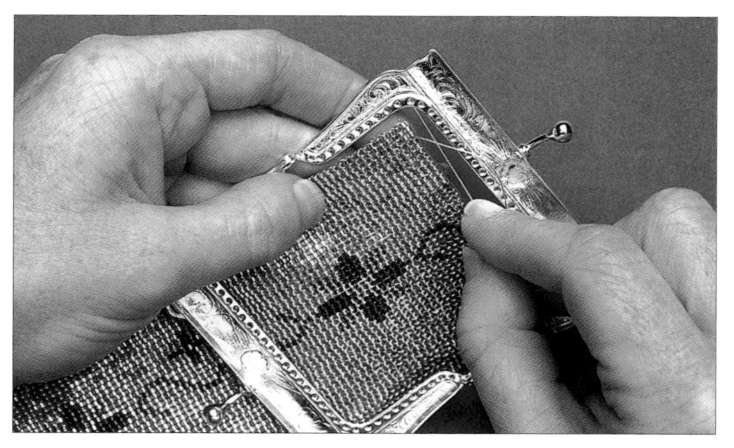

2. Thread the needle with nymo and weave it into the beadwork. Bring the needle out through the third bead from the left-hand corner. Line up the centre of the pattern on the panel with the clasp on the frame. Push the needle through the first hole in the frame.

3. Take the needle back through the second hole in the frame and then through two more beads. Sew the length of the top edge in this way.

4. Now sew the right-hand side of the purse to the frame. Finish off by weaving the thread into the beading. Snip off any excess thread.

Tip

You may wish to make this purse using different beads. If so, bear in mind that your beadwork must measure 7.5cm (3in) to fit the 7cm (2¾in) purse frame. Make a test line of beads before you begin and adjust the number of warps accordingly.

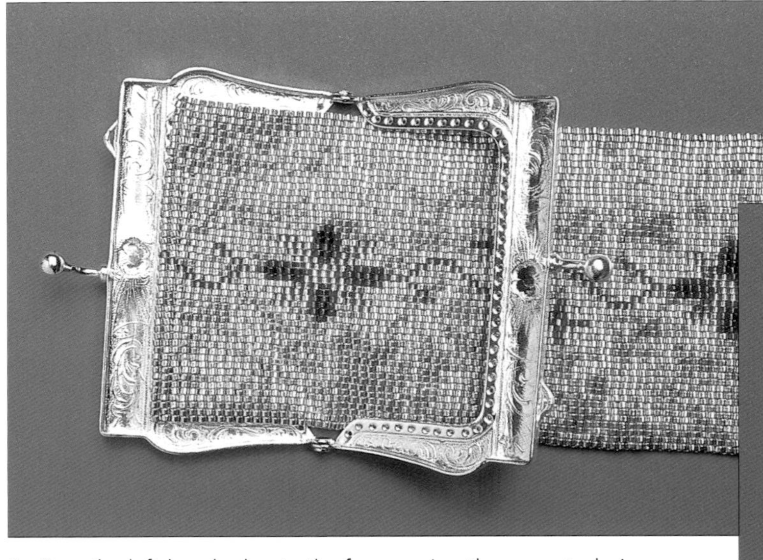

5. Sew the left-hand edge to the frame using the same technique.

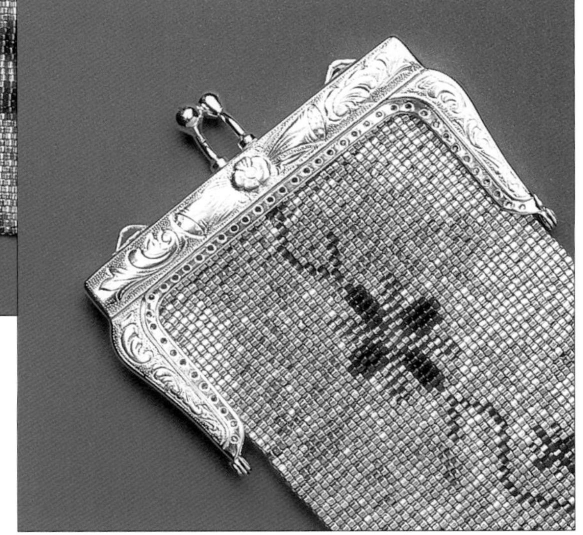

6. Now fold the panel in half and sew the beadwork to the frame, as described in steps 2–5.

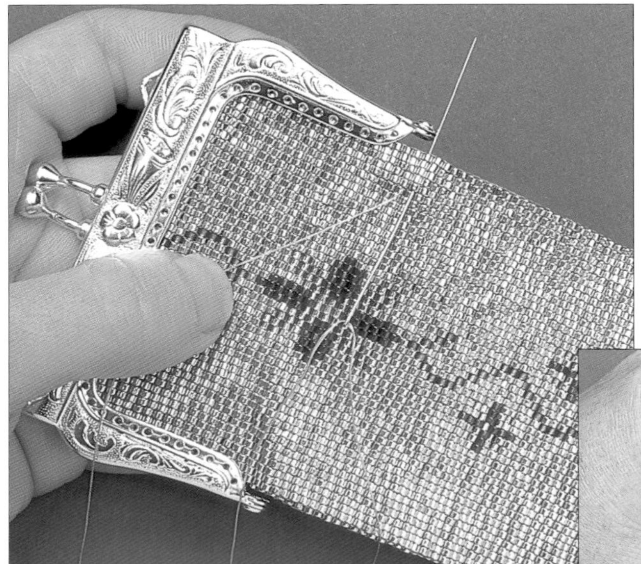

7. Fasten a new thread to the beadwork and bring the needle out on one side at the row of beads beneath the hinge. You must allow a gap, and not sew right up to the frame, so that the purse can open and close easily.

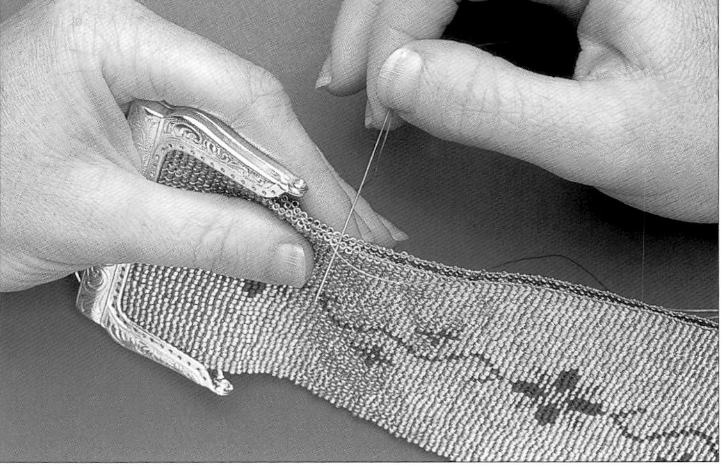

8. When sewing up the sides, push the needle in and out of the weft threads, not through the beads. When you have completed both sides, feed the needle through the beadwork to fasten the thread.

The finished purse. If you wanted to, you could thread a long string of beads to make a bead strap and then wear this purse over the shoulder.

Bugle beads are good for making striking patterns. You will always be able to find this coin purse in your bag.

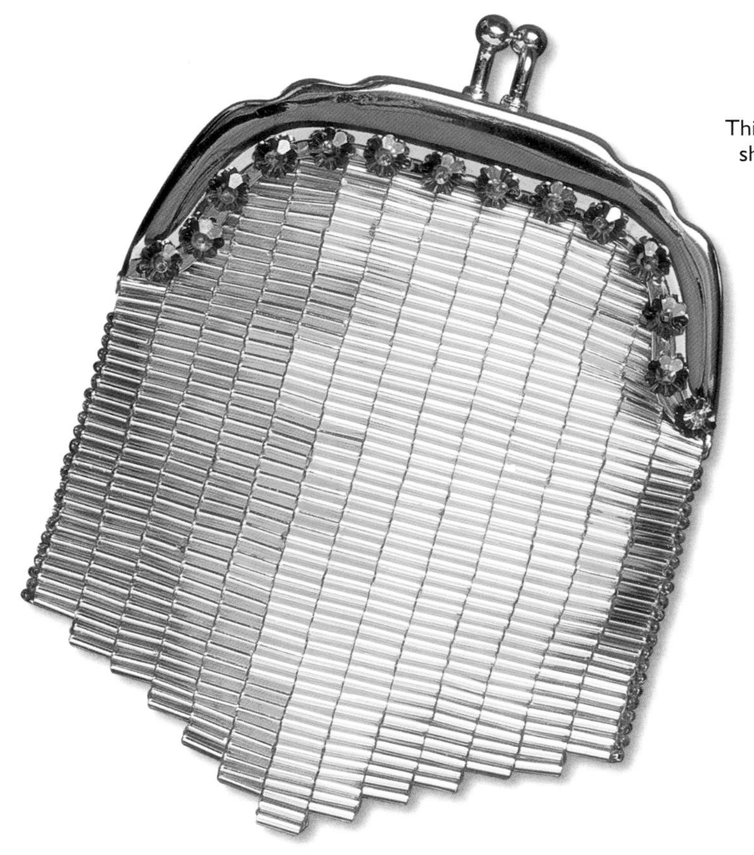

This variation on the purse opposite shimmers like gold and shows that one colour can have real impact.

I attached these twinkly marguerites as I sewed the beading to the frame. Each time I came up through a hole in the frame, I picked up a marguerite and a seed bead, brought the needle back through the marguerite and then went down through the next hole.

Mermaid Madeleine

Beading on a loom does not have to feature repeat patterns, you can bead almost any picture. This pretty door hanging will give an aquatic feel to your bathroom or a special little girl's bedroom. I have used a free-hand weaving technique called spiral stitch to make the wonderful, twisty hanger.

You will need

Beginner's loom

Nymo, white

Loom beading needle, size 12

Beading needle, size 10

Beads for the panel, delica:

- Green mix 27 plus D373 – 18g (for panel and fringe)
- Pink satin D833 – 10g
- Matt cream D353 – 3g
- Beige satin D674 – 1.5g
- Gold D34 – 1g
- White D66 – 12g
- Red D602 – 8 beads
- Blue D47 – 8 beads
- Peach D54 – 13 beads

Beads for the fringe:

- 6 Vitrail drop crystals
- 6 Yellow shell sequins
- 4 Cast gold dolphins

Scissors

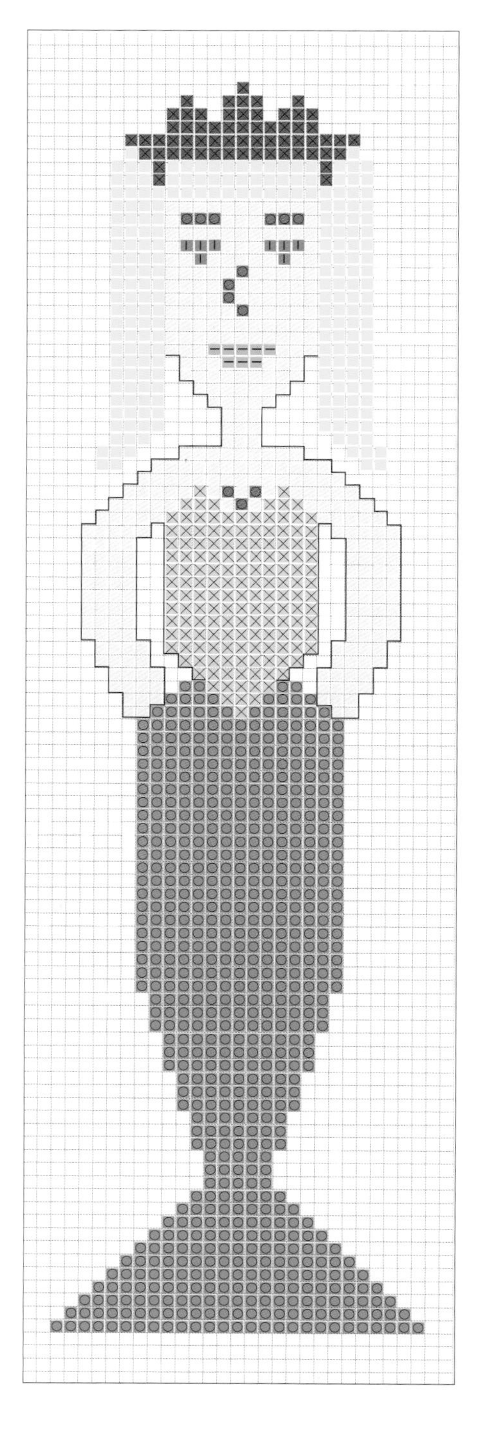

- White
- Beige satin
- Gold
- Blue
- Matt cream
- Red
- Peach
- Pink satin
- Green mix

Overall size: 5 x 37cm (2 x 14½in)

The panel has 104 rows of 31 beads.

In this pattern, every square represents a bead. Follow the colour key below as you work.

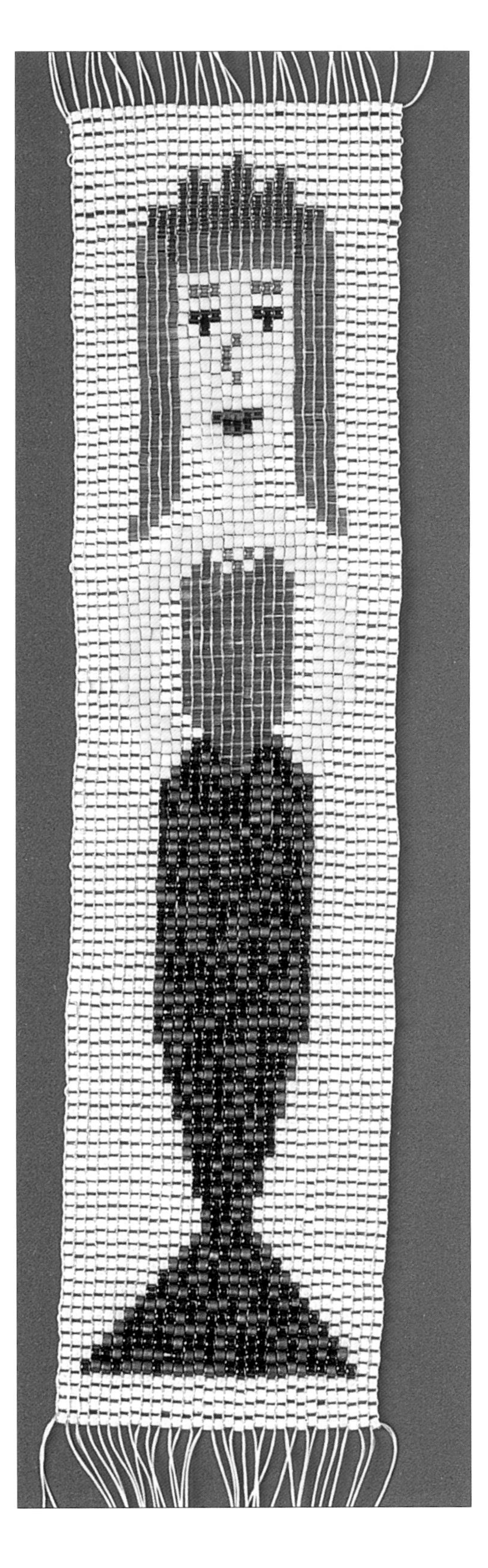

1. Set up the loom with 32 nylon warp threads. Then, following the pattern opposite, weave the mermaid panel. Cut the finished panel off the loom.

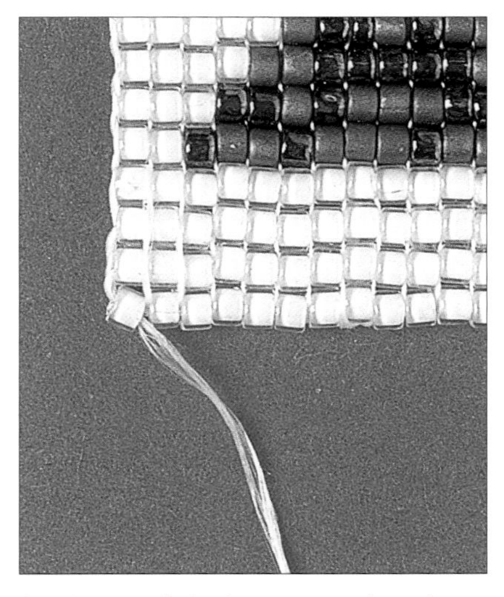

2. Weave all the loose warp threads into the beadwork. Thread the needle with a new length of thread, weave it into the beadwork to exit, left to right, through the bottom left-hand bead.

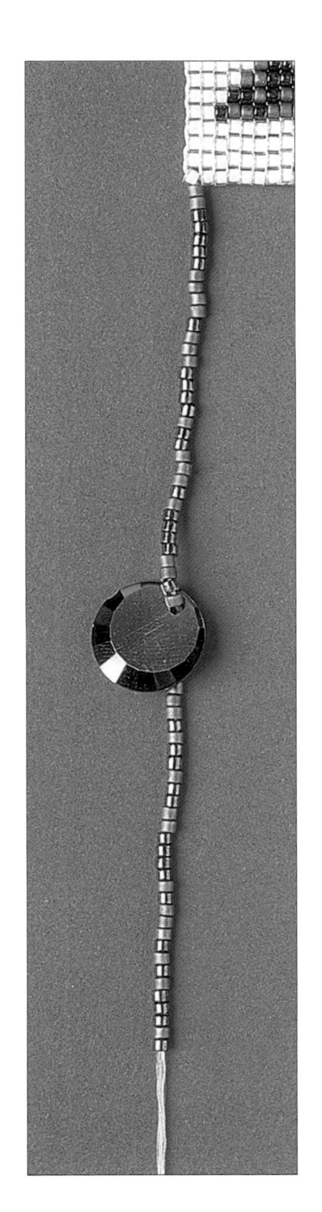

3. Pick up 35 mixed green beads, one flat crystal and another 35 mixed green beads. Push them up to the bottom of the panel.

4. Twist the thread between your thumb and forefinger a number of times. Do not let go!

5. Still holding the thread tightly just below the last bead, take the needle, left to right, through three beads at the bottom left-hand corner of the panel.

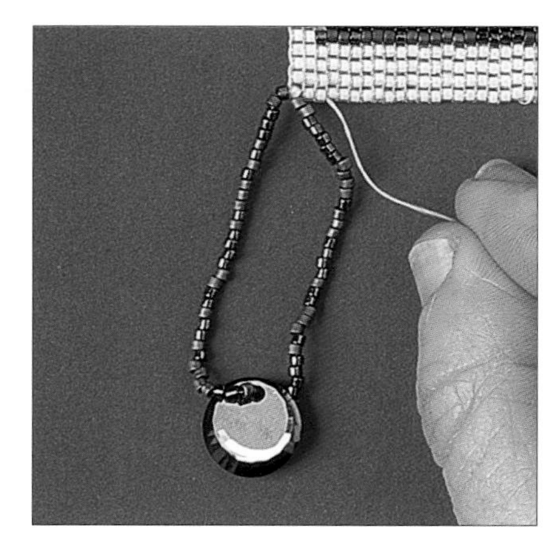

6. Continue to hold the beaded thread firmly as you pull the loose end of the thread through. Keep pulling until the beads meet the bottom of the panel.

7. Pick up the flat crystal and allow the two lengths of beads to twist around each other.

8. Repeat steps 3–7 to make fifteen more tassels along the bottom of the panel, adding either a sequin, charm or flat crystal to each one. With each new tassel, increase the number of seed beads that you pick up by ten. After the ninth tassel, decrease by ten.

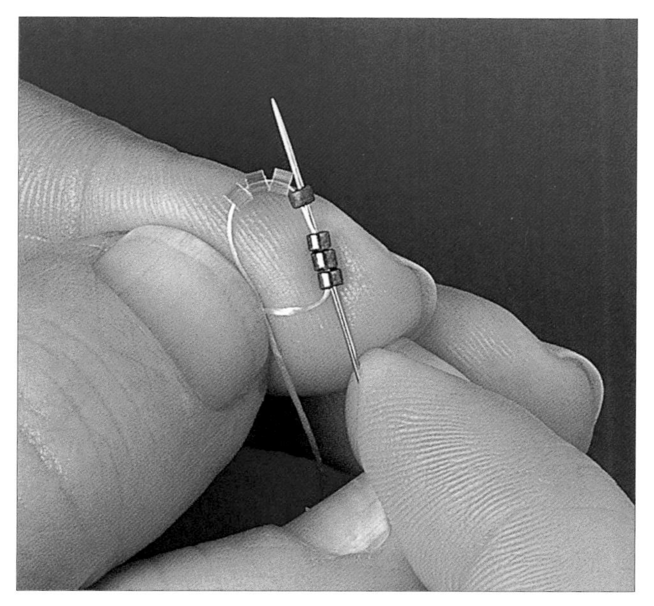

9. Now start the spiral rope for the hanger. Thread the needle with a 1m (39½in) length of nymo – you may need more to complete the spiral rope but a piece any longer than this may tangle, see 'Tip' below. Pick up four mixed green beads and three pink satin beads, bring the needle round to form a loop and push the needle back through the four green beads.

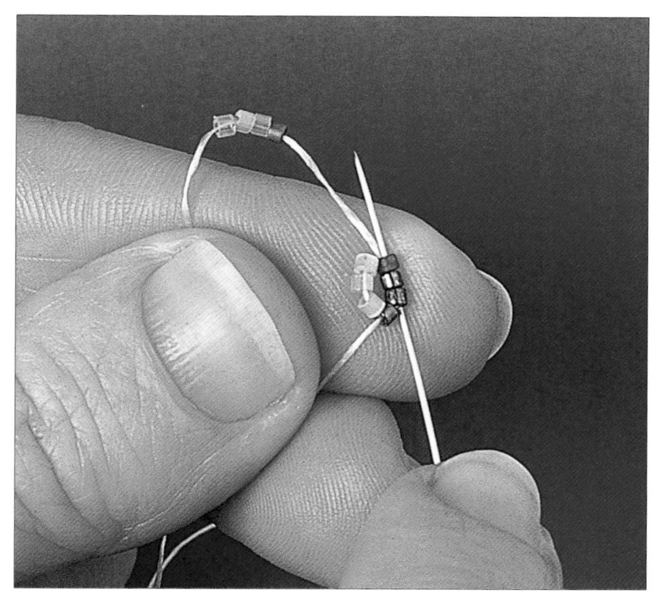

10. Close the loop and pick up one green bead and three pink beads. Bring the needle round and back through the top three of the previous four green beads.

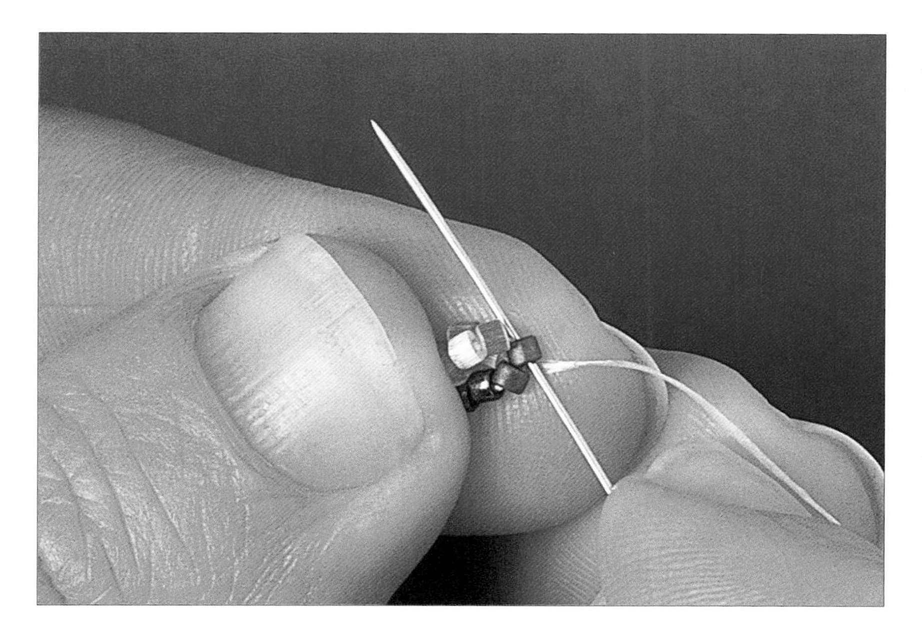

11. Pull the thread through and then take the needle through the new green bead that you added in step 10.

Tip

When you have 7cm (2¾in) of thread left, bring a new thread through three of the green beads. Knot the two threads together. Thread the tail of the old thread on to a needle and work it back into the beading. You can snip off the tail of the new thread.

12. Repeat steps 10–11 until the rope is 41.5cm (16½ in) long.

13. Using the working thread on the end of the spiral rope, take the needle, left to right, through the left-hand bead in the second row up from the bottom.

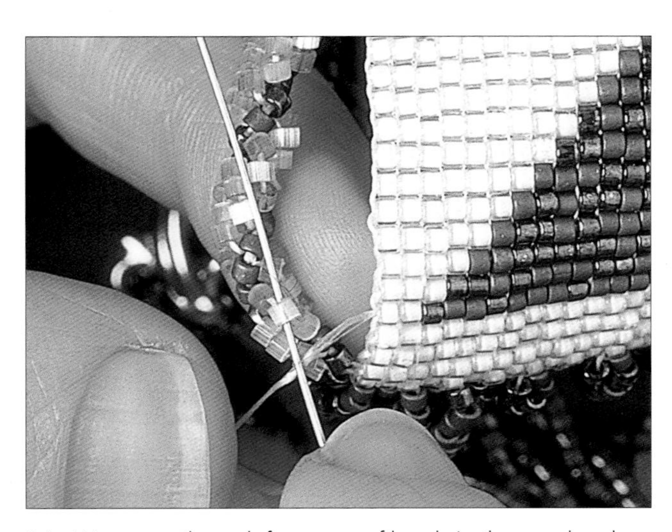

14. Weave up through four rows of beads in the panel and exit on the left-hand side at the fourth end bead. Now take the needle through the middle bead in the three-bead spiral closest to the needle.

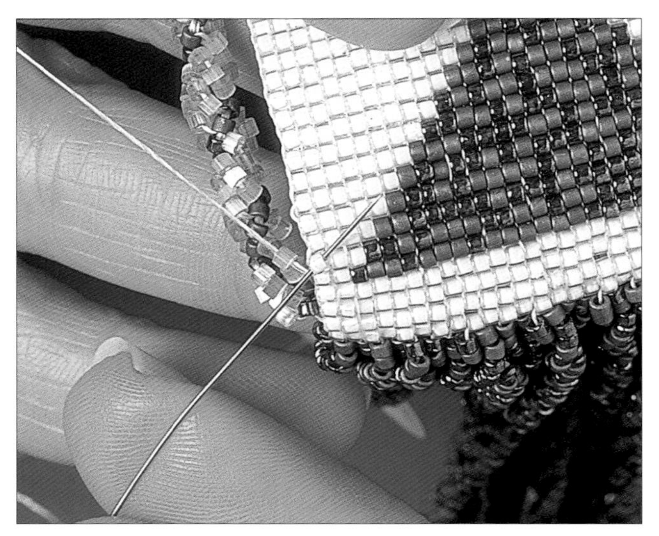

15. Take the needle, left to right, through the end bead in the sixth row.

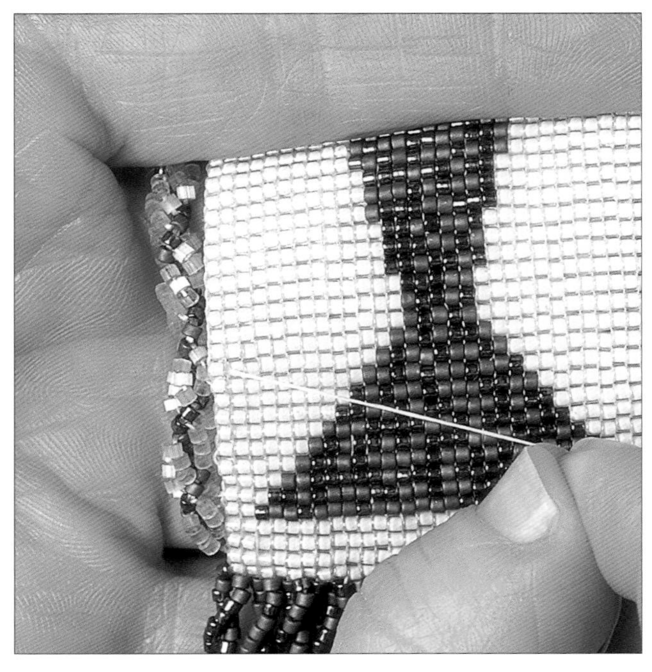

16. Pull the thread tight, then repeat steps 14–15, but, this time weave up through eight rows of beads.

17. Continue stitching the spiral to the left-hand side of the panel in this way until you reach the top and then weave the end of the thread into the panel. Working up from the bottom, repeat steps 13–16 to attach the spiral to the other side of the panel. You should end up with a loop at the top of your panel.

The twisted tassels on Mermaid Madeleine look like seaweed swaying under the ocean giving a lovely, watery effect.

This little purse is bee-lightful! If you extend the width it would make a terrific clutch bag.

Opposite
This tulip bag has a glorious leafy fringe.

Christmas Sparkle

When it gets close to Christmas, beading something festive is a must in my house. I wanted this bauble design to be simple, sleek and modern and I have used a split-loom technique to achieve the effect.

You will need

Beginner's loom

Nymo, red

Beading needle, size 10

Beads, red LBC37 – size 10. 2/cut (hex) 10g

Scissors

Plastic/glass silver bauble 5.5cm (2in) diameter

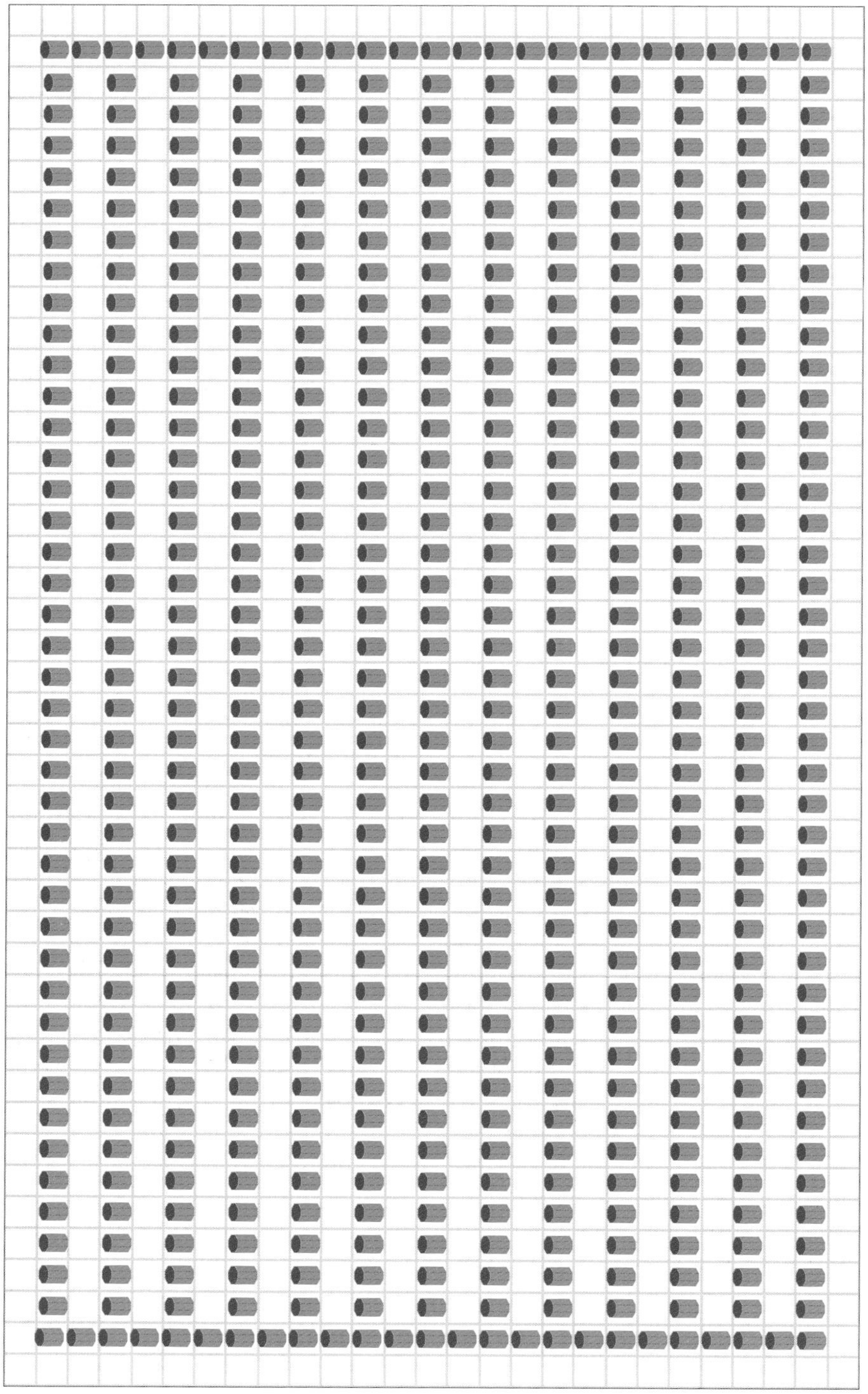

Each coloured square represents a bead.

Size: 8 x 5.5cm (3¼ x 2¼in)

1. Warp up with 26 threads and set up a row of 25 beads across the weft approximately 3cm (1¼in) down from the separators. Leave a long, loose tail at the left-hand side – see the picture beside step 6, overleaf.

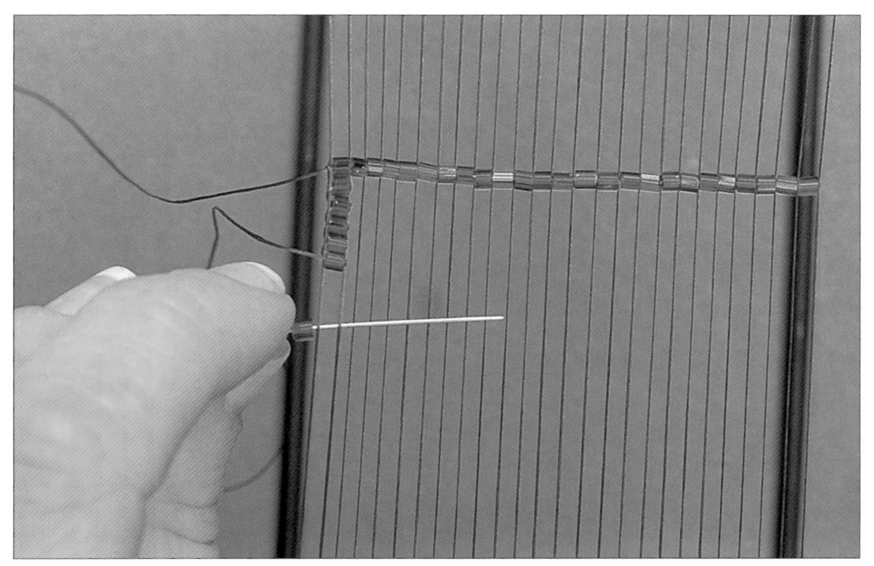

2. To create the first vertical column, pick up a bead and pass the needle under the first two warp threads.

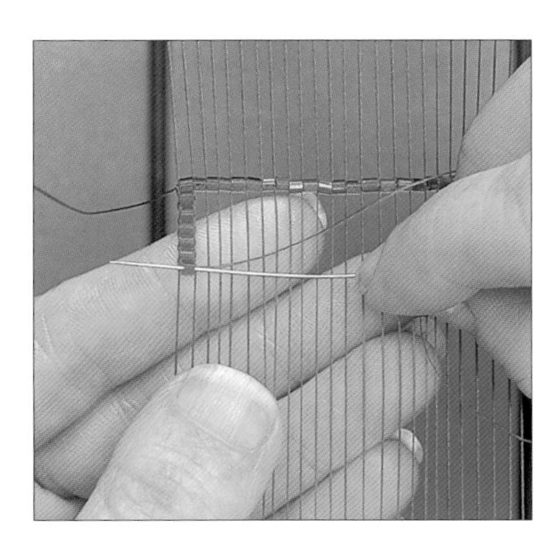

3. Position the bead between the warp threads, bring the needle round and pass it through the bead above the warp threads. Continue working backwards and forwards in this way, adding a new bead each time until you have a column of 40 beads.

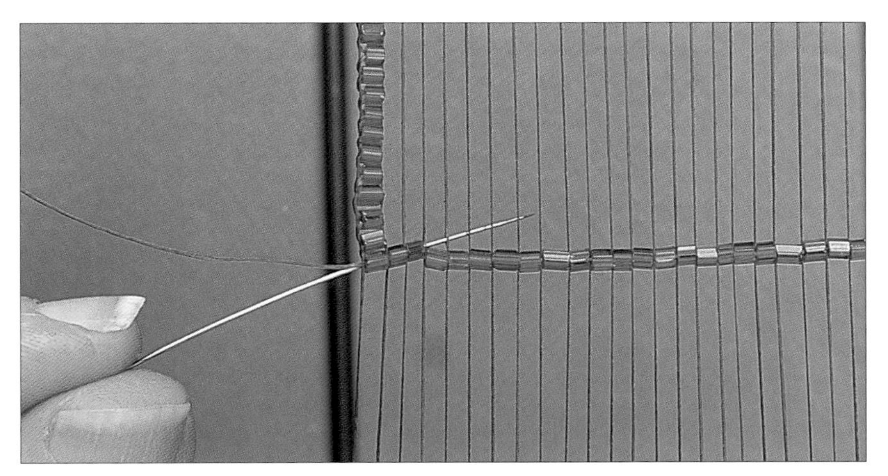

4. Now add a horizontal row of 25 beads. When you bring the needle back out on left-hand side, you must feed it under the loop connecting the last two beads in the column. Pull the thread tight and then push the needle back into the row and out through the third bead.

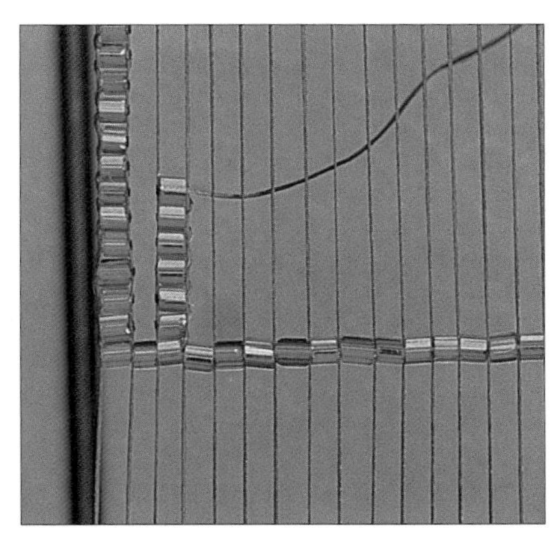

5. Weave back and forth adding a bead at a time as before to create the second vertical column. Continue adding columns until you have 13 in total. If you start to run out of thread at any point, weave what remains back and forth into the beading and use the same technique to start a new thread.

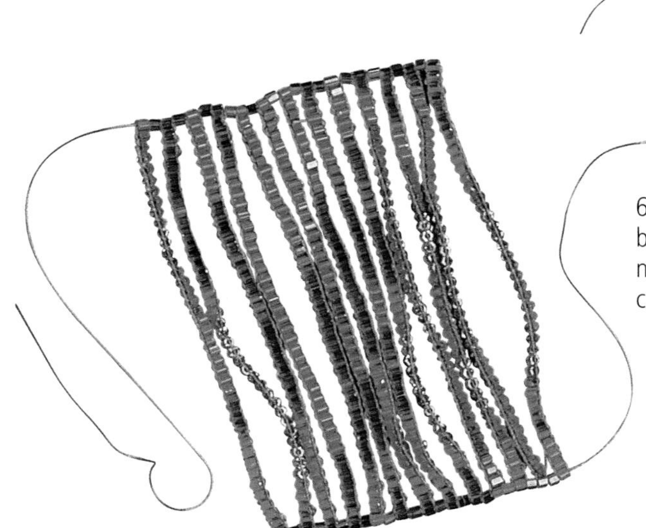

6. Complete the beading and finish off but do not trim off the excess thread. You need long, loose threads at opposite corners of the beading as shown here.

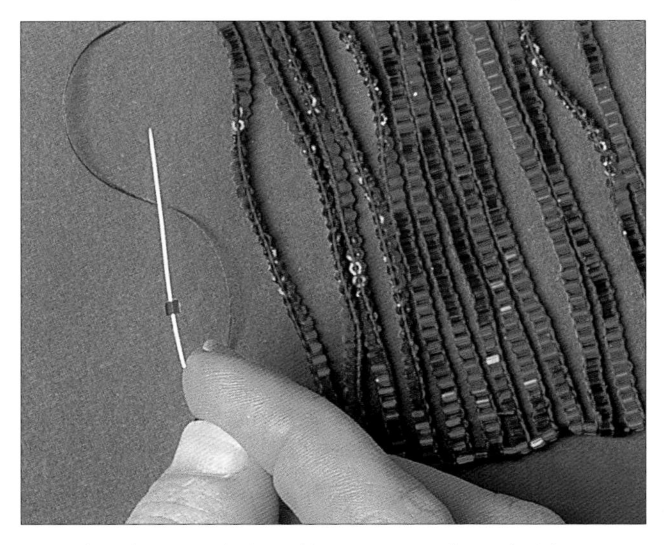

7. Take a loose end, thread it on to a needle and pick up a bead.

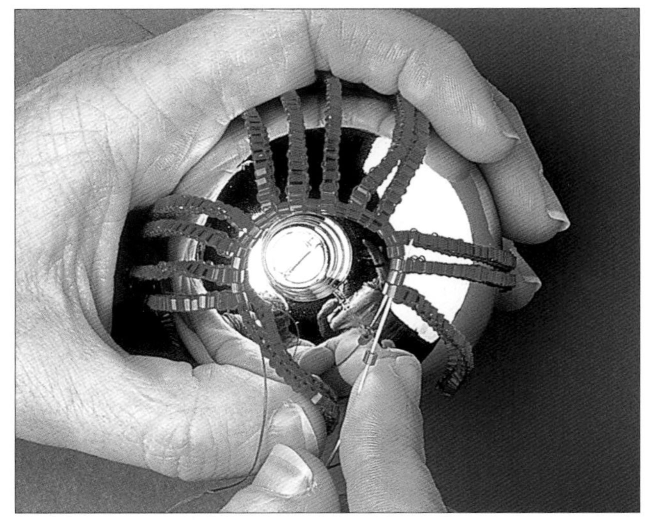

8. Wrap the beading around the bauble so that the corners of the panel meet. Push the needle through the bead on the opposite corner.

9. Sew the two corners together. Finish off by going back and forth with the needle down one of the rows.

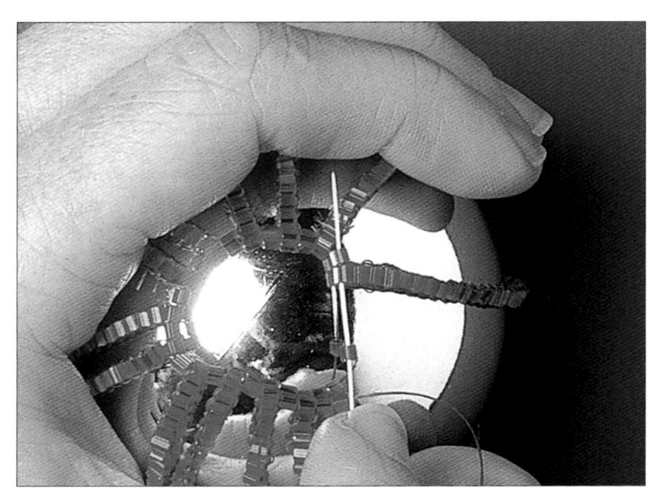

10. Repeat steps 7–9 at the bottom of the bauble.

You will have the best dressed Christmas tree in the neighbourhood with these baubles. The smaller bauble was made using the split-loom technique but I added swags and drop crystals between the vertical rows.

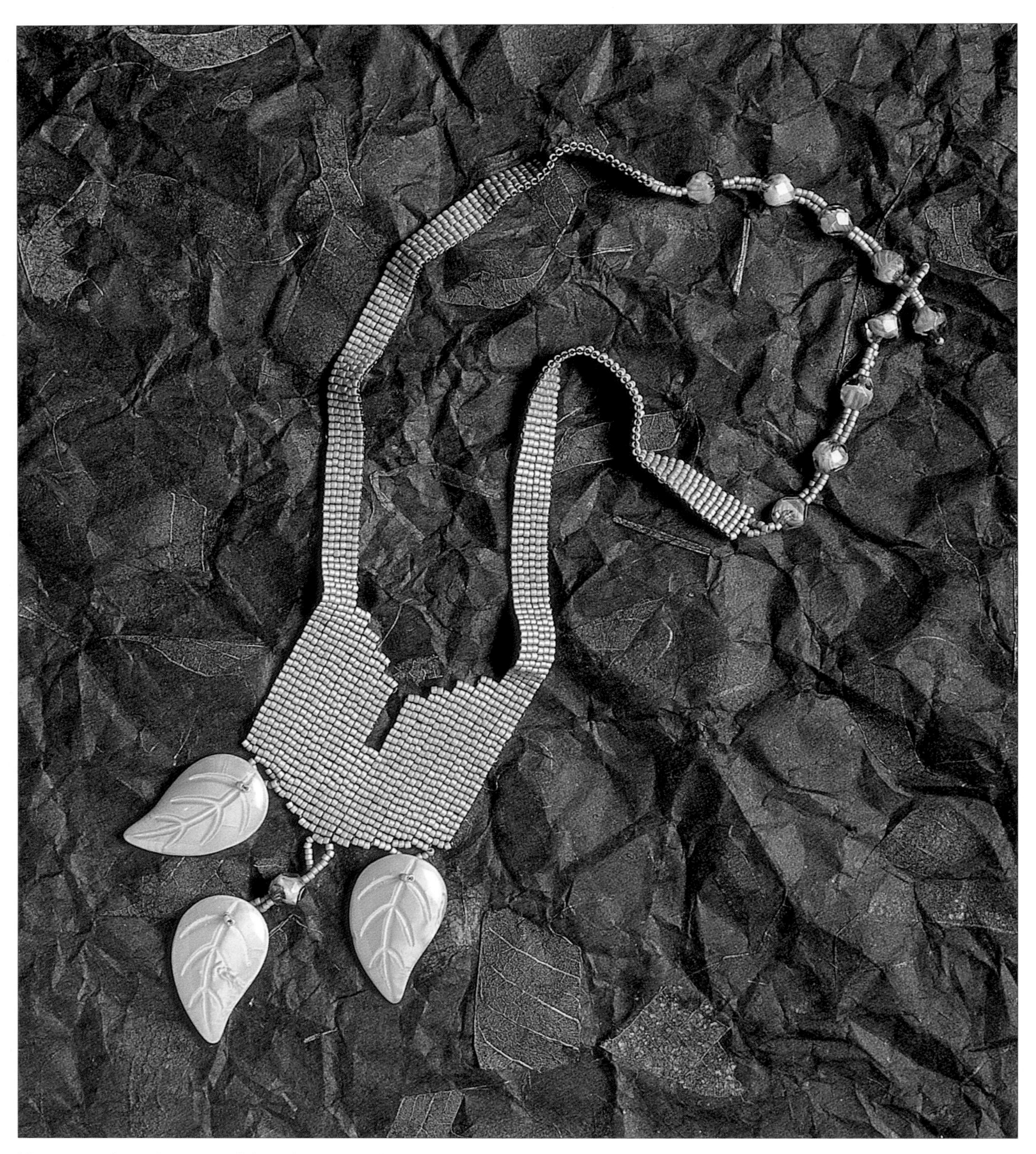

Here is another adaptation of the split-loom technique. Plain beadwork really sets off the unusual, decorative beads.

Opposite
This necklace is simplicity itself, just embroidery thread and five panels of beads.

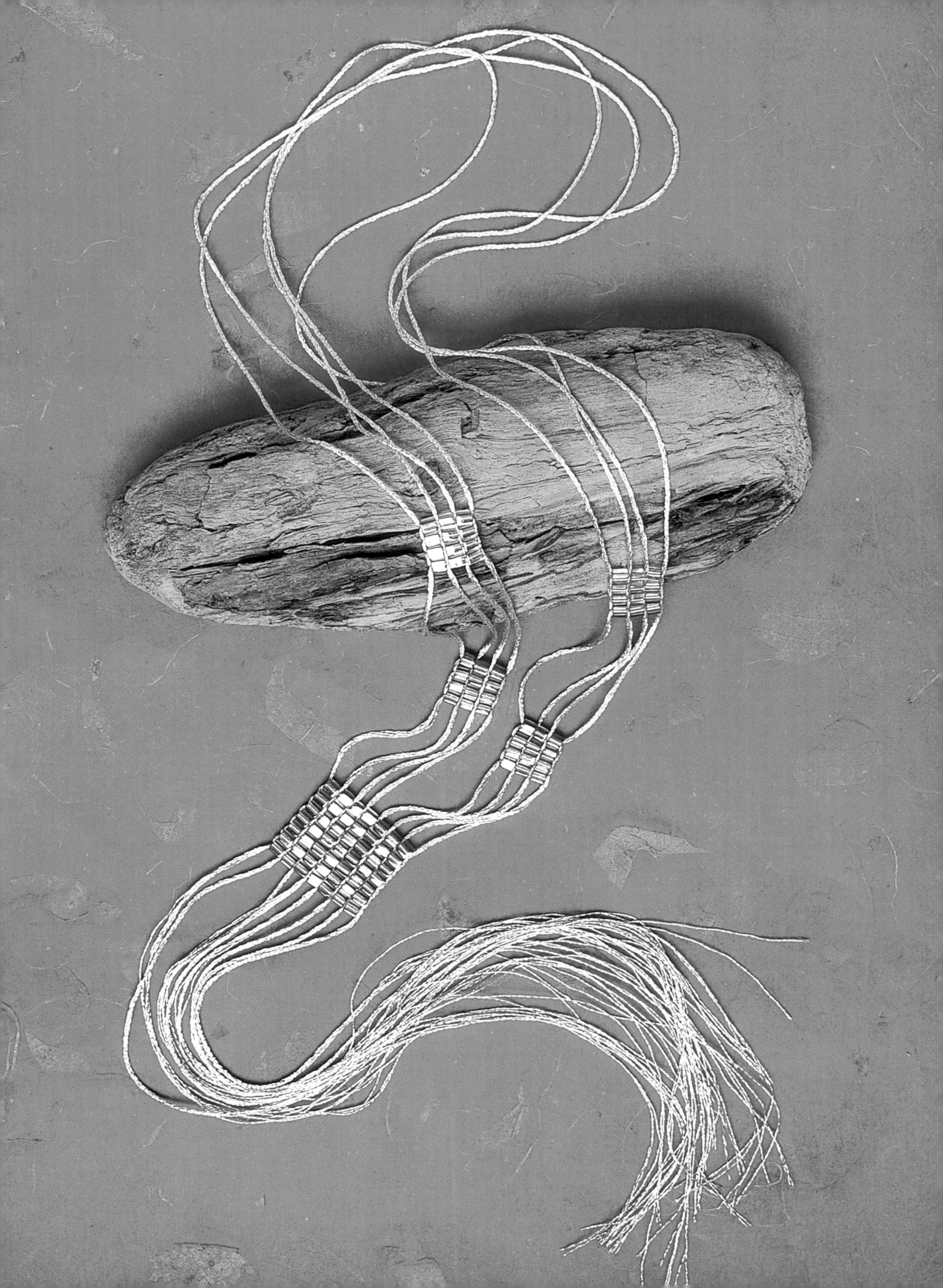

Winter Games

This miniature draughtboard will help you while away a rainy afternoon. Make the board on a loom and then follow the steps to make each of the pieces. This draughts set will be small enough take on a journey but you will need a steady surface to play on!

You will need

- Large 41cm (16¼in) double-sided upright loom
- Nymo, white
- Loom beading needle, size 12
- Beading needle, size 10
- Beads for the board, delica:
  - Matt silver lined, DB221 – 7g
  - Opaque white AB, DD202 – 7g
  - Black, DB010 – 7g
  - Matt black, DB310 – 7g
  - Red, DB603 – 4g
- Austrian crystals for the pieces:
  - Jet cubes (12x8mm)
  - Jet squashed (12x6mm)
  - Crystal AB cubes (12x8mm)
  - Crystal AB squashed (12x6mm)
  - Headpins x 24
- Scissors
- Round-nosed pliers
- Side-cutters

Red

Matt black

Black

Opaque white

Matt silver lined

Size: 11.5 x 11.5cm (4½ x 4½in)

The panel has 68 rows of 84 beads.

Each square represents a bead. Follow the colour key.

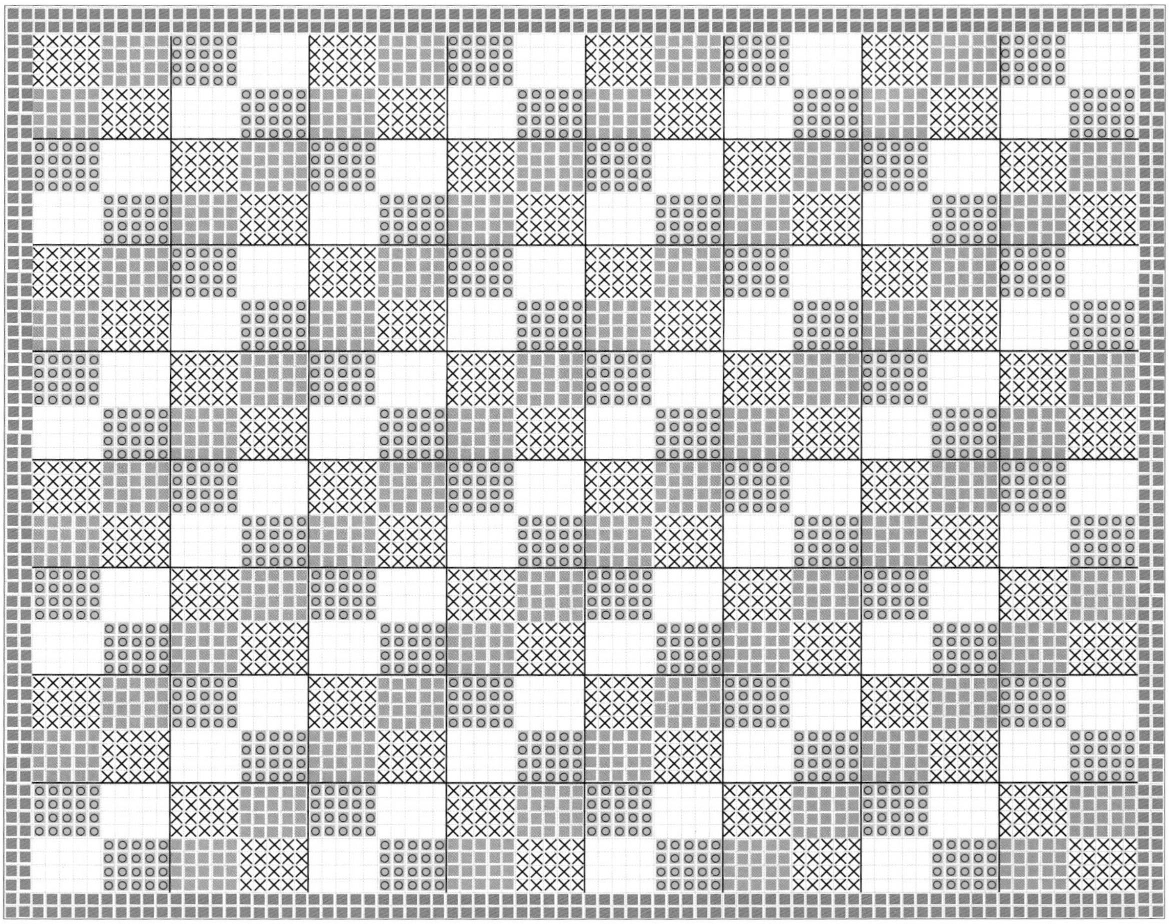

1. Warp your loom with 85 threads and bead two rows of red delicas. Start the third row with two red delicas and then begin to build up the draughtboard. Follow the pattern opposite carefully as you pick up your beads. When you have completed the beading, cut it off the loom and finish off all the threads.

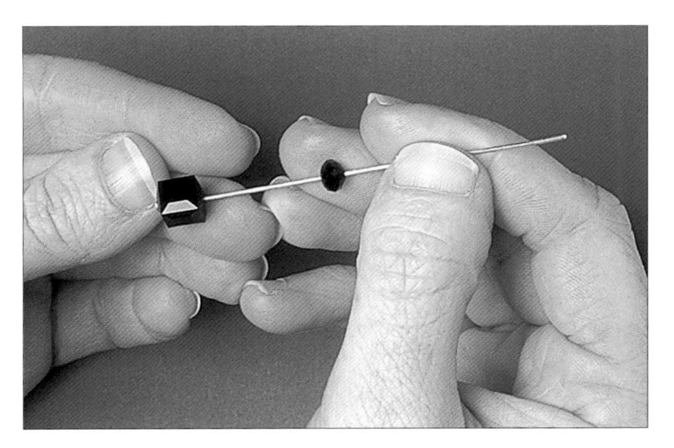

2. Thread a jet cube crystal and then a jet squashed crystal on to a headpin.

3. Cut the pin with side-cutters, leaving 1cm (3/8 in) above the squashed crystal.

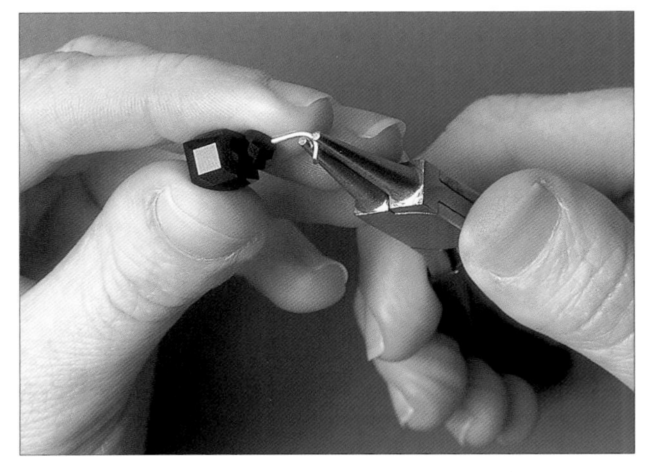

4. Turn the end of the pin into a loop using round-nosed pliers.

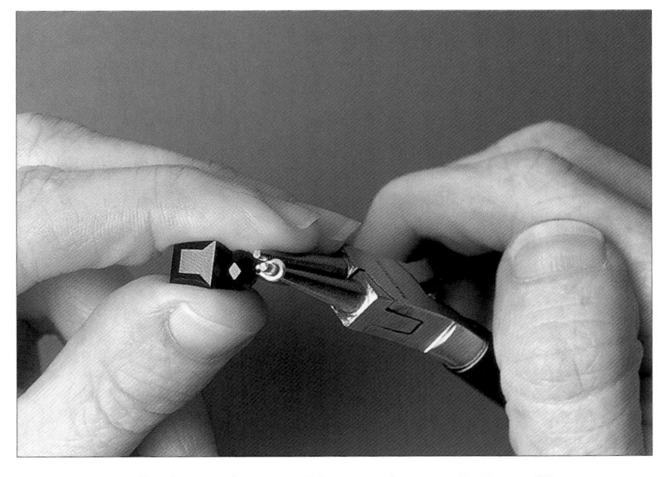

5. Even up the loop shape with round-nosed pliers. Now repeat steps 2 to 4 to make 12 black draught pieces and 12 clear crystal draught pieces in the same way.

This miniature draughts set is the perfect present for the man who has everything.

If chess is more your game, experiment with different combinations of crystals to create the castles, knights, bishops, pawns, king and queen. Make one set of playing pieces from clear crystal cubes and jet crystals and make the opposing team from clear crystal cubes and red crystals.

Dream Weaver

Uneven beads give this five-panelled wall hanging a pretty surface. As with the braided belt on page 32, I have incorporated interesting threads into the design. They are left long at the bottom of the beading to be seen in all their glory. Hang this piece beside a window and watch the threads move in the breeze.

You will need

- Large 41cm (16¼in) double-sided upright loom
- 22 variegated textured threads, dusty pink, 140cm (55¾in)
- Nymo, dusty pink
- Loom beading needle, size 12
- Beading needle, size 10
- Seed beads, size 8, 180g mixture of grey Ceylon, AB mauve transparent and dusty pink Ceylon
- Round crystals (2x10mm)
- Scissors
- Epoxy glue
- Wooden dowelling, 46cm (18in), diameter 1cm (3/8in)

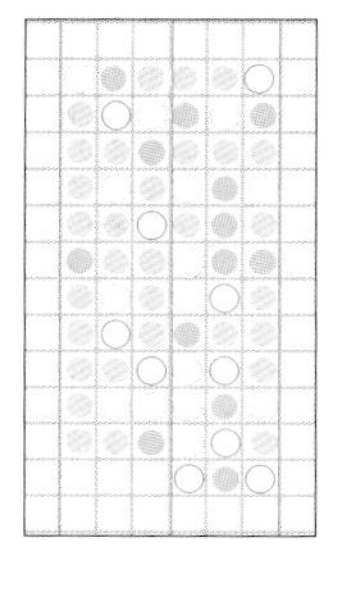

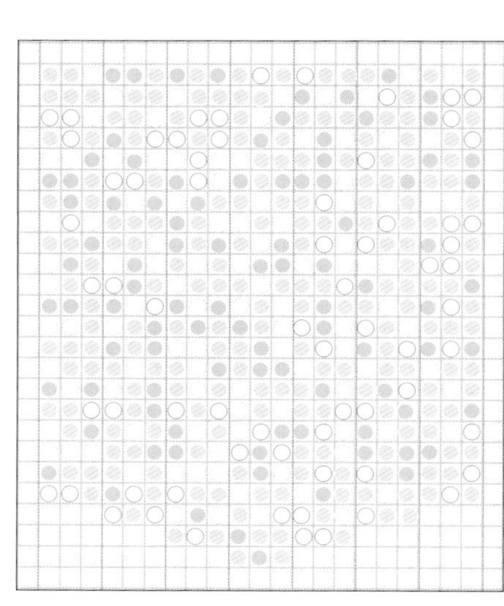

Each coloured square represents a bead but the pattern is random.

Overall size:
48 x 32cm (19 x 12½in)

The large panel has 42 rows and they start to decrease after row 32. Follow the diagrams for each of the three panels as you bead.

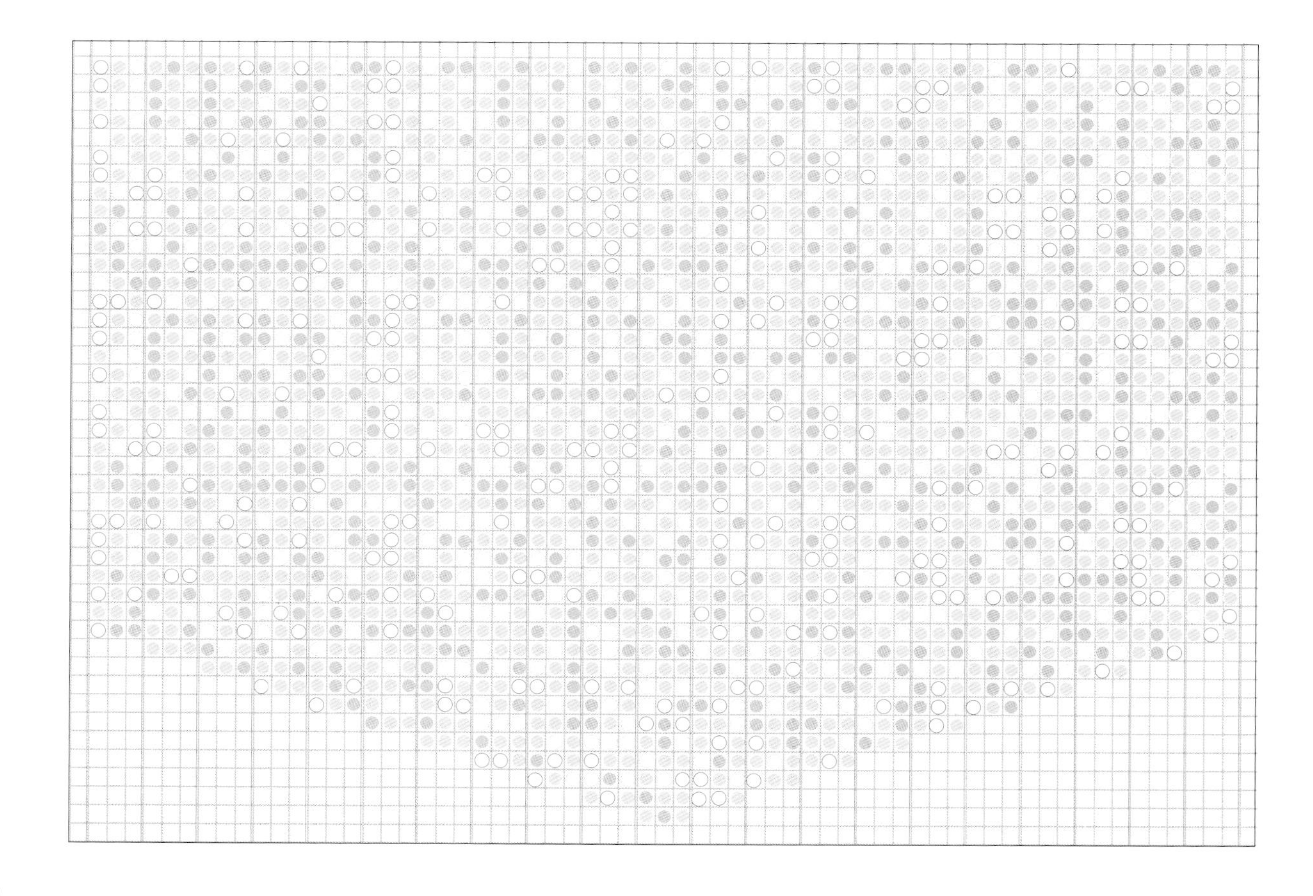

1. Tie the 22 lengths of warp thread to the loom. Keep the mix of colours and textures random. Leave at least 20cm (7¾in) of thread at the top of the loom and about 30cm (11¾in) at the bottom.

2. Thread your needle with nymo and referring to the pattern on the opposite page bead the first row of the large panel on the front warp. Place this row approximately ten centimetres down from the separators. Select the beads at random to create a textured effect and set three beads between each warp thread.

Tip

Shake a small pile of beads out on to your beading mat and scoop up a random mix of colours with your needle.

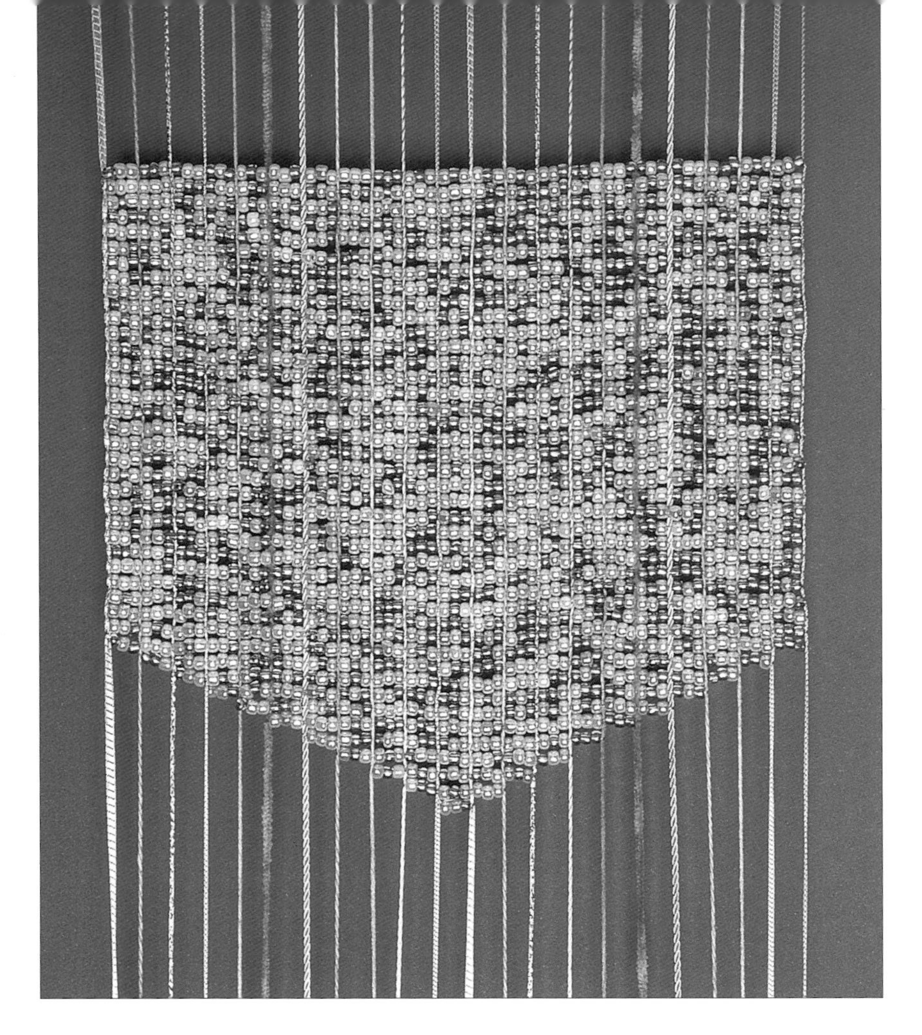

3. Bead 32 rows. From row 33 onwards, decrease by three beads at each end until you reach a row of just three beads. Secure the thread by feeding it back into the rows above, then snip off any excess.

4. Now bead two medium and two small panels on the back warp. Weave the medium panel across eight warp threads with three beads between each warp. After 21 full rows start decreasing as shown in the diagram on page 60. Weave the small panels across three warp threads with three beads between each warp. Bead 11 full rows then decrease one row by three beads.

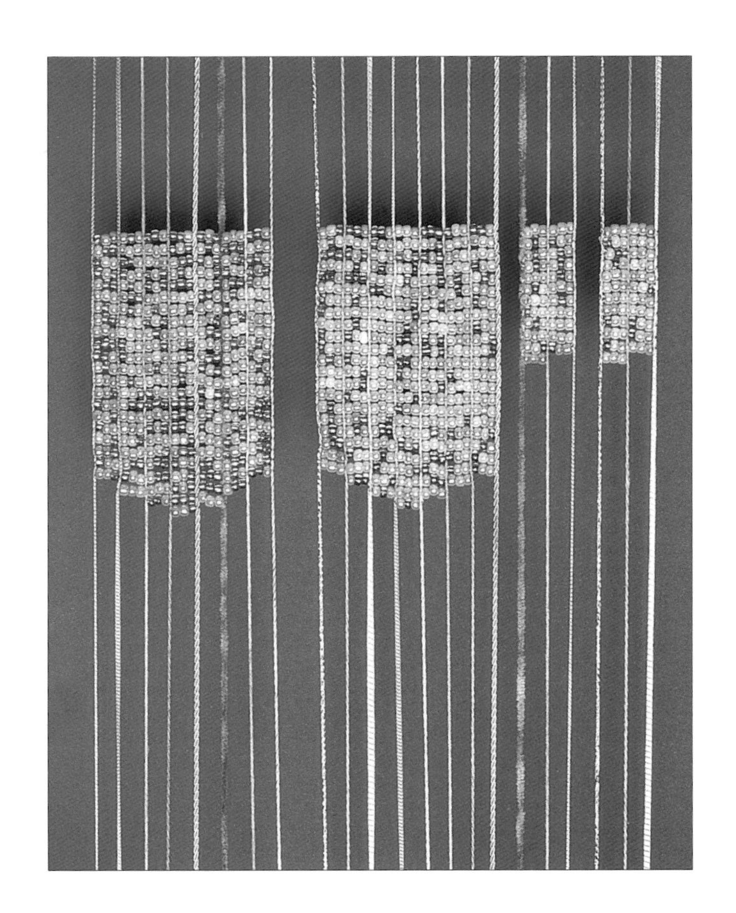

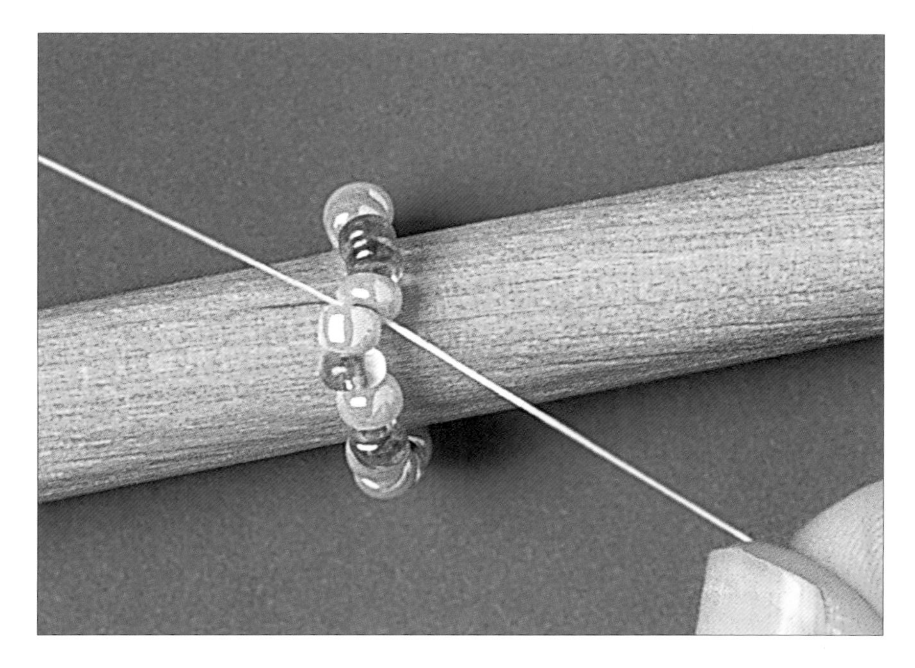

5. Now begin to bead around the wooden dowelling with tubular Peyote stitch. First, cut a 1m (39½in) length of thread and then thread the beading needle and pick up sixteen beads. You must pick up an even number of beads even though this may not result in a snug fit. It is better to add an extra bead and work slightly loose, than remove one and create gaps between beads. Tie a double knot.

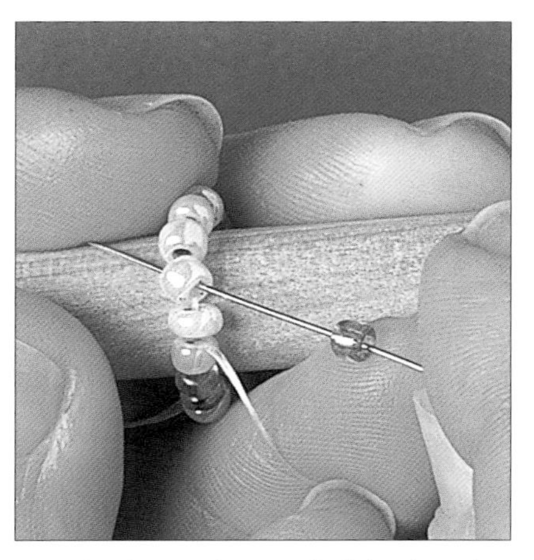

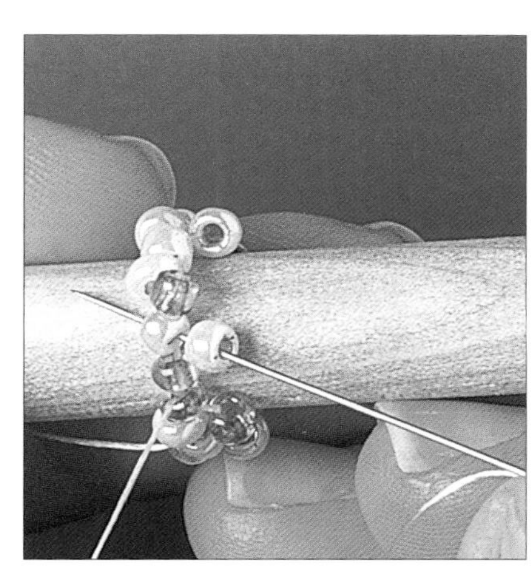

7. Pick up another new bead and take the needle through the next-but-one bead on the dowel. Repeat with another six beads to arrive back at the start point.

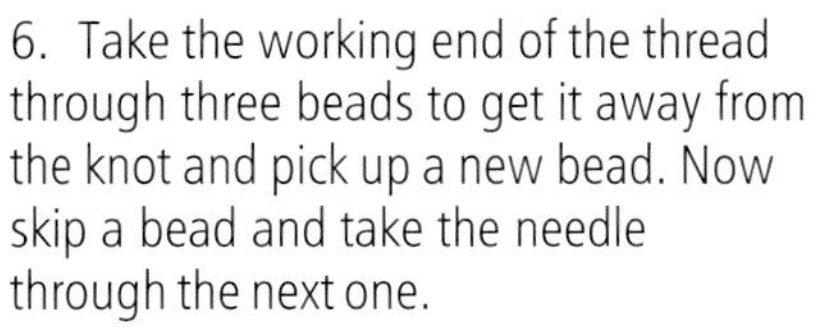

6. Take the working end of the thread through three beads to get it away from the knot and pick up a new bead. Now skip a bead and take the needle through the next one.

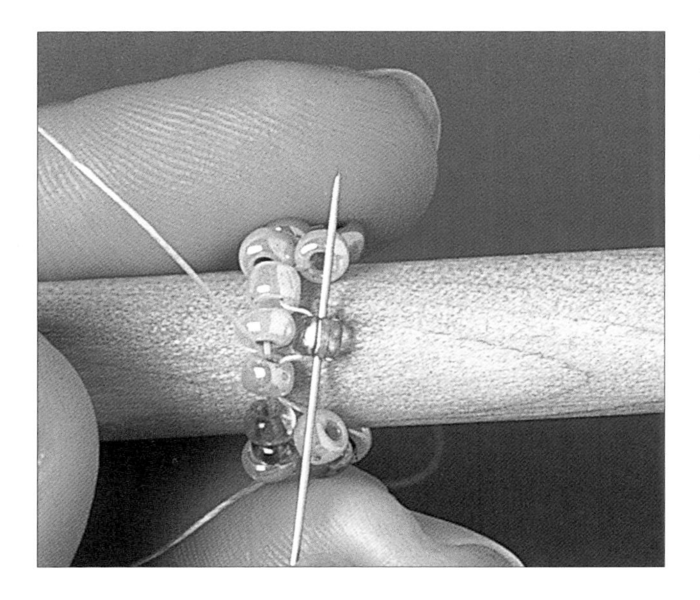

8. Pull the thread through. Then, without picking up a bead, take the needle through the first bead in the gappy row that you have just created. This is called stepping up.

9. Continue building up the stitch, picking up a bead and passing the needle through the next-but-one bead each time. Work eight beads per row and step up at the end of each row.

10. Bead the length of the dowelling rod making sure that two rows of beads extend over each end.

Tip

Arrange several piles of eight beads on your beading mat before you start adding rows to the dowelling rod. Each pile represents a row, making it easy to tell where one row ends and another begins. Once you have used all eight beads, you will know that it is time to step up.

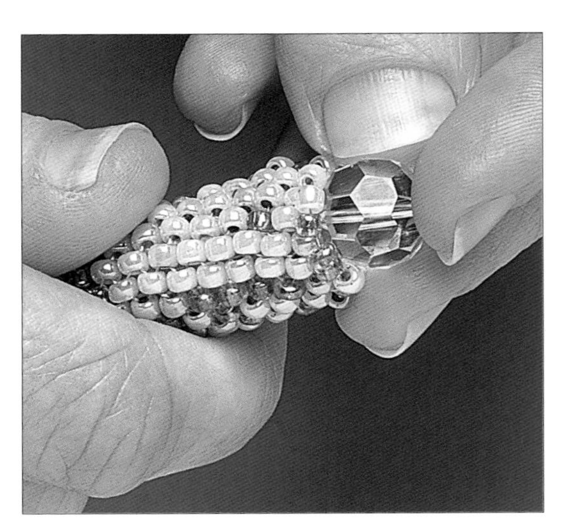

11. Use epoxy glue to attach a large crystal to each end of the wooden dowelling.

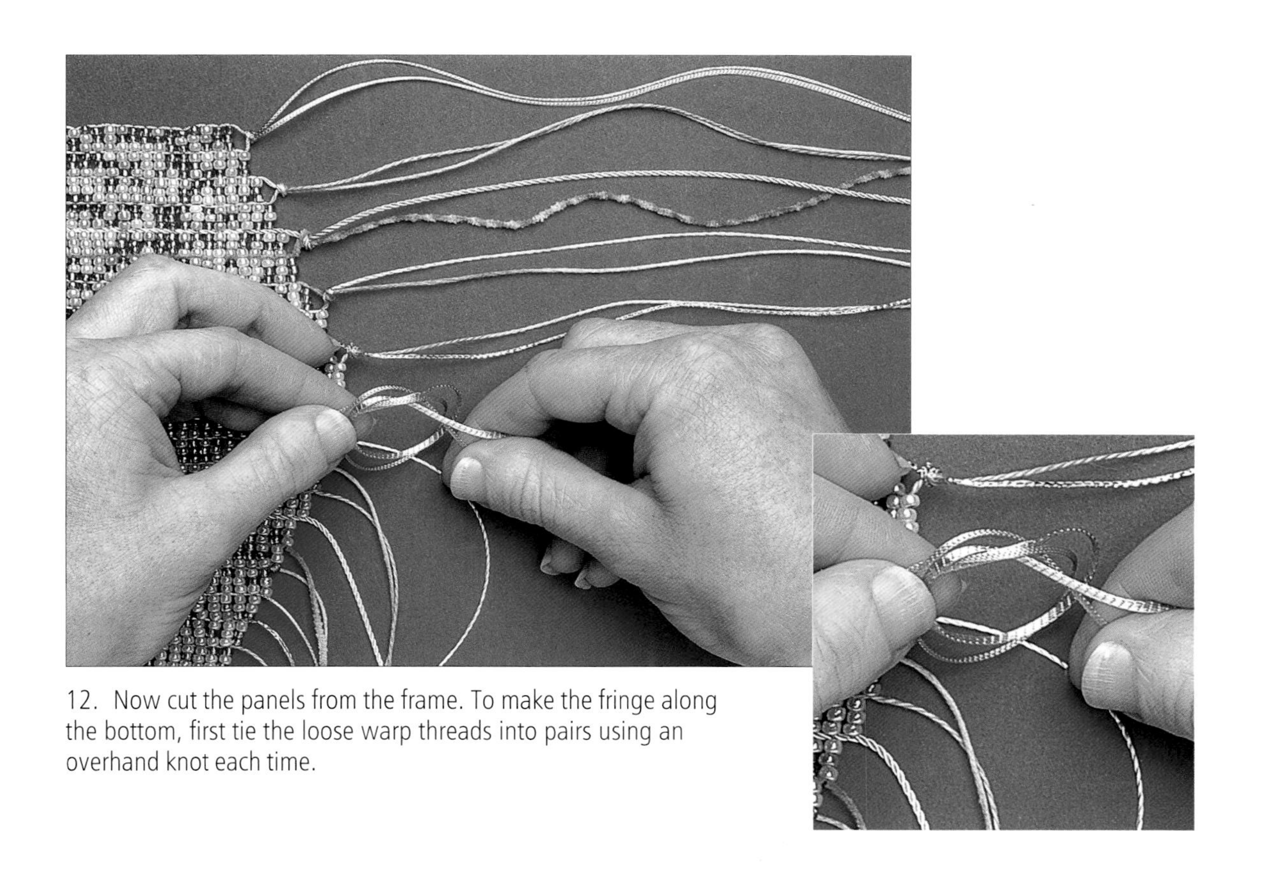

12. Now cut the panels from the frame. To make the fringe along the bottom, first tie the loose warp threads into pairs using an overhand knot each time.

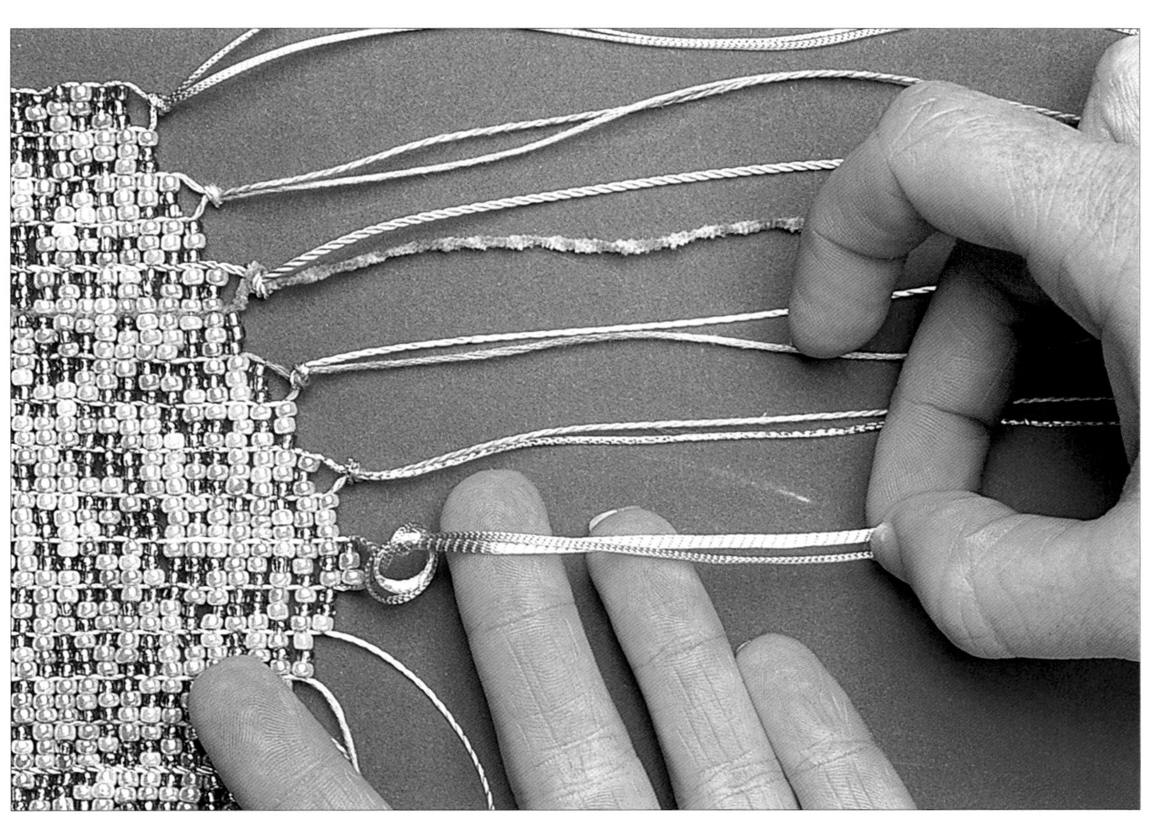

13. Now pull each pair of threads with one hand and push the loop along with your other hand so that all the knots are tight to the bottom of the panels.

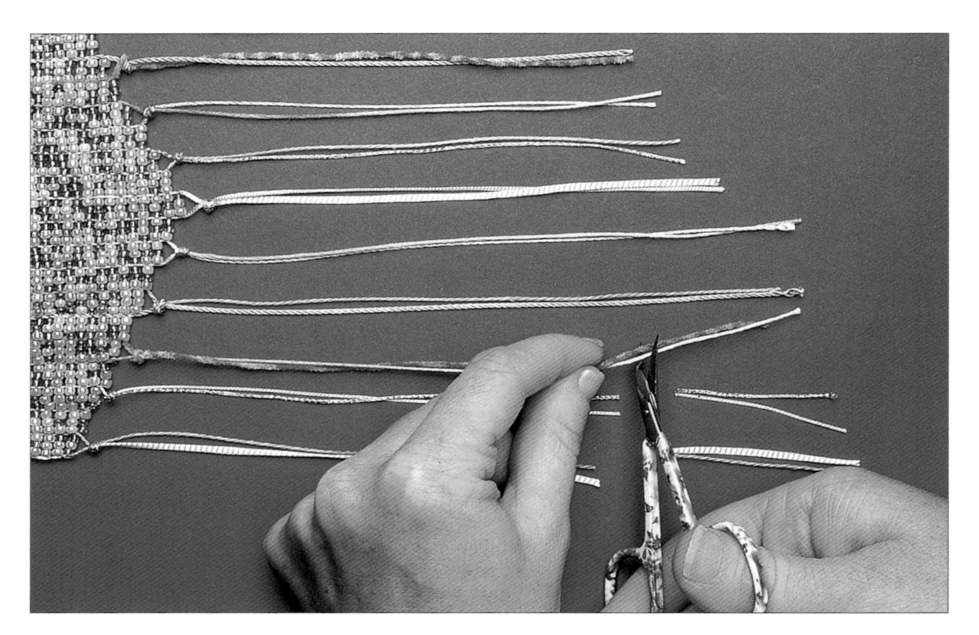

14. Next, decide how long you want the pair of threads in the middle of the fringe on the large panel. Then, working from the middle out, create a slant on one side by snipping each pair of warp threads slightly shorter than the previous pair by increments of approximately 5mm (¼in). Repeat on the other side.

15. Knot and trim the fringes on the smaller panels in the same way. If you are uncertain how long you want the fringe, it is best to trim off just a small amount. If you then decide you want the fringe to be shorter, you can always trim away more. Line up the five panels and space them out along the wooden dowelling.

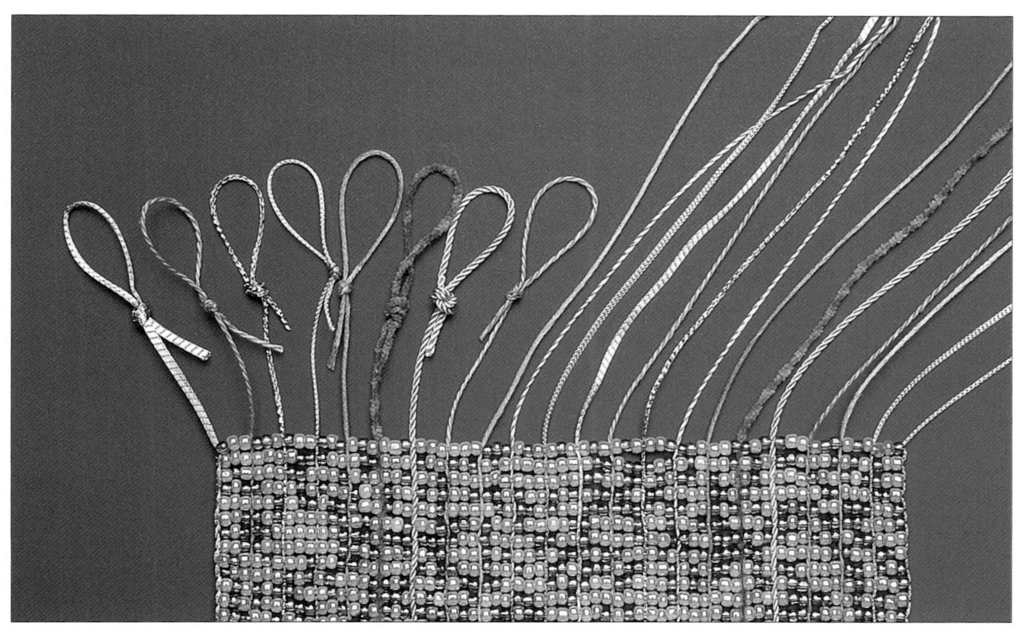

16. Tie a loop on each warp thread along the top of all five panels. Try to make the loops as evenly sized as possible.

17. Select a length of textured thread to use as the hanger and tie a loop at each end.

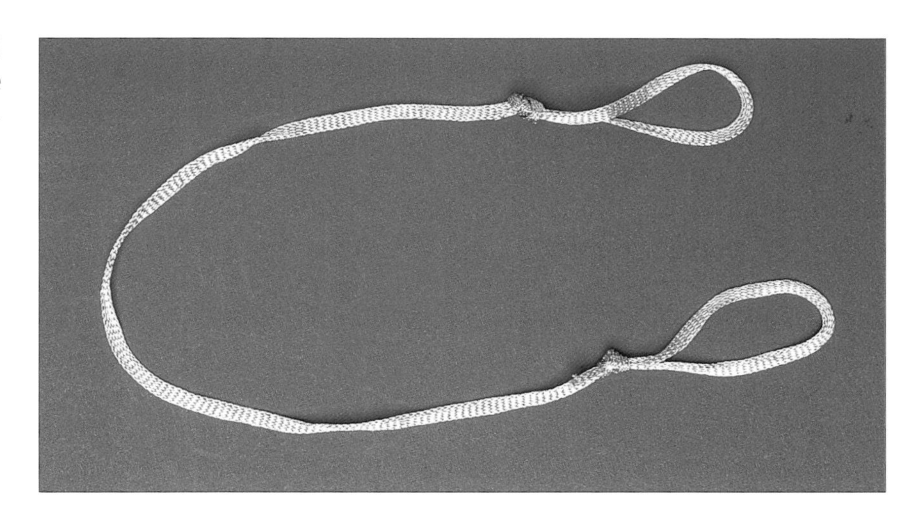

18. Finally, feed the dowelling rod through the loops on the panels and hanger in this order: small, medium, hanger loop, large, hanger loop, medium, small.

This wall hanging really shows off your handiwork. Hang it up with pride.

Above

Hang this up in the window and on a sunny day, it will throw sparkles around the room. Suction cup hangers are available from craft shops.

Cupid's Bag

Just because your loom is rectangular it does not mean that your beadwork needs to be! You can experiment with all kinds of exciting shapes once you have learnt to decrease the number of beads on the loom. This is an easy skill to learn and very liberating.

You will need

Continuous warp loom
Nymo, dusty pink
Beading needle, size 10
Beads, delica:
- Pink DDB902 – 24g
- Metallic purple DDB12 – 24g
- Metallic silver DDB35 – 5g

Scissors

Each coloured square represents a bead.

Size: 9 x 11cm ($3\frac{1}{2}$ x $4\frac{1}{2}$ in)

The bag has 37 rows of differing lengths. Follow the pattern, and the list below, as you decrease the beads.

From this row down:

6 rows 31 beads
1 row 29 beads
1 row 28 beads
2 rows 25 beads
3 rows 22 beads
3 rows 19 beads
2 rows 16 beads
2 rows 13 beads
2 rows 10 beads
2 rows 7 beads
2 rows 5 beads
2 rows 3 beads
1 row 1 bead

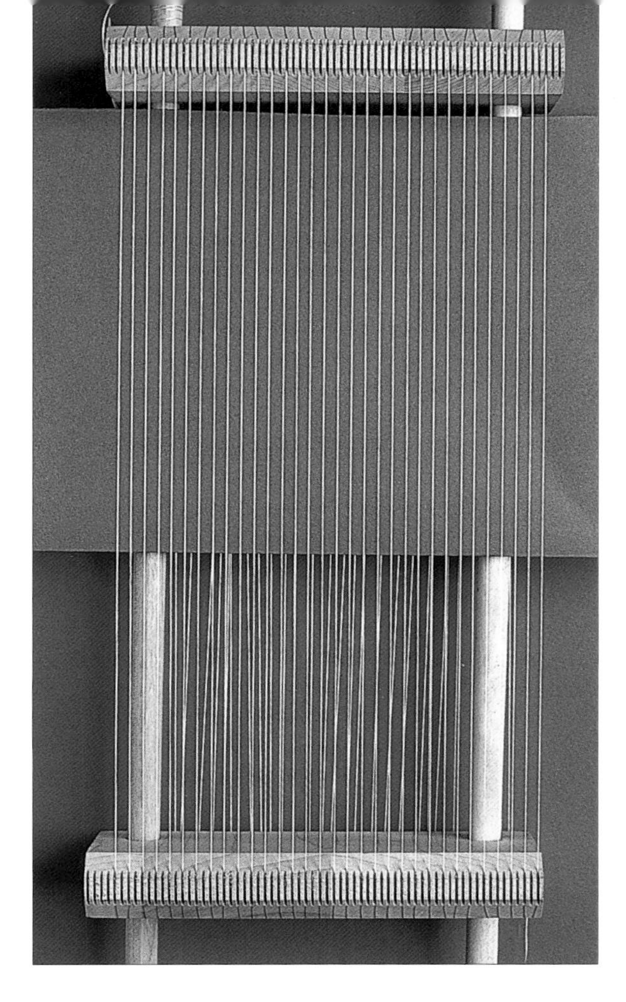

1. Warp your loom with 32 warp threads. This particular loom allows me to wind the warp with one continuous length of thread, taking it over and under the separators. It is an alternative method of warping up that produces two warps, one on the front and one on the back. Here, I have placed a piece of paper between the warps so that only the top warp threads are visible.

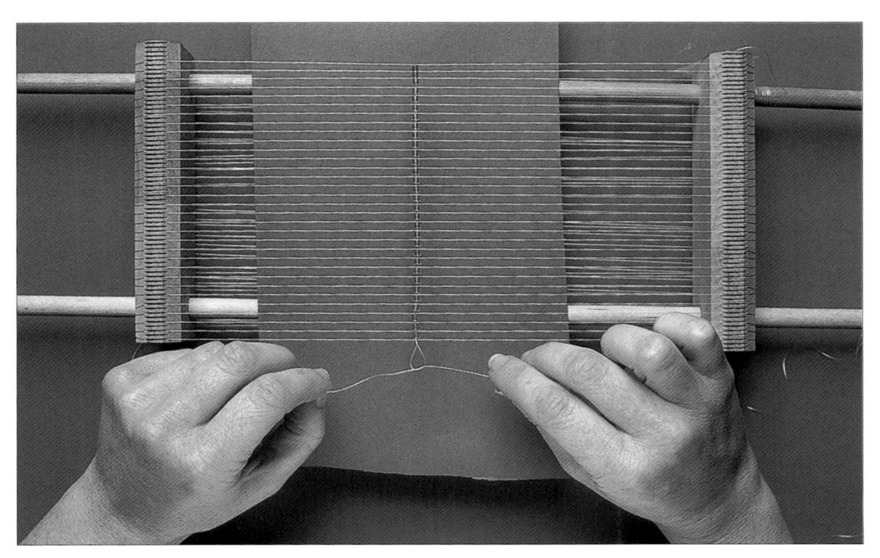

2. Use an overhand knot to tie a 1m (39½in) length of nymo to the warp, approximately half way along. Thread the needle with 31 pink beads, pass the thread under the warp, place the beads between the warp threads and bring the needle back through the beads. Remove the needle from the thread, undo the knot and tie both ends of the weft together.

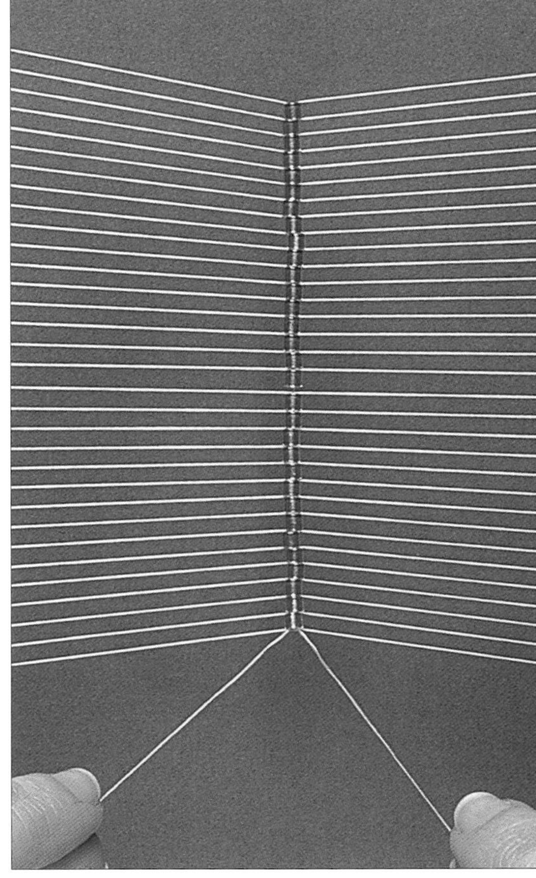

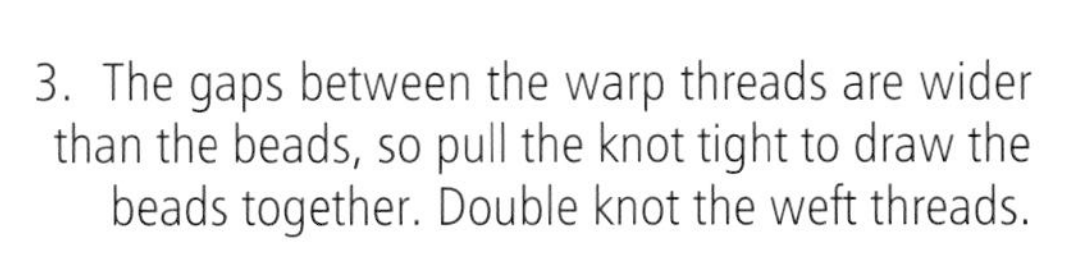

3. The gaps between the warp threads are wider than the beads, so pull the knot tight to draw the beads together. Double knot the weft threads.

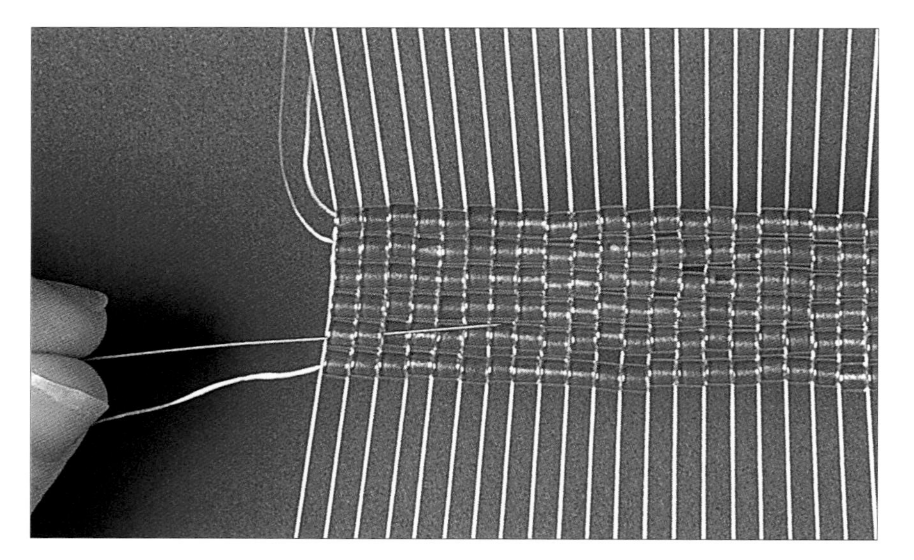

4. Weave another five rows of 31 beads. To secure the sixth row before you start decreasing, feed the needle through the first two beads (left to right) on the row above.

5. Pull all the thread through. Now feed the needle right to left through the second bead in the sixth row and take the needle down between the left-hand warp threads (follow the arrow).

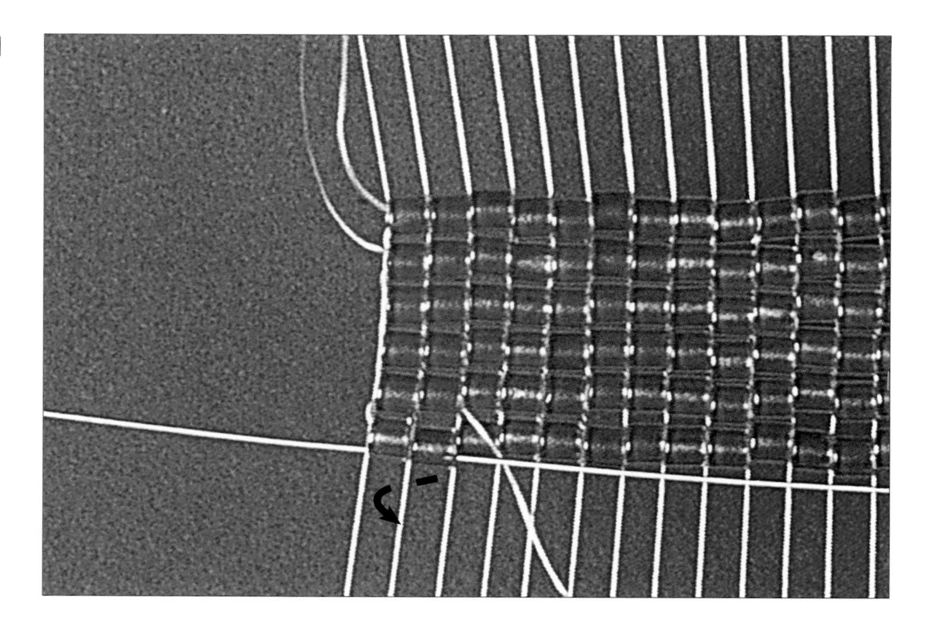

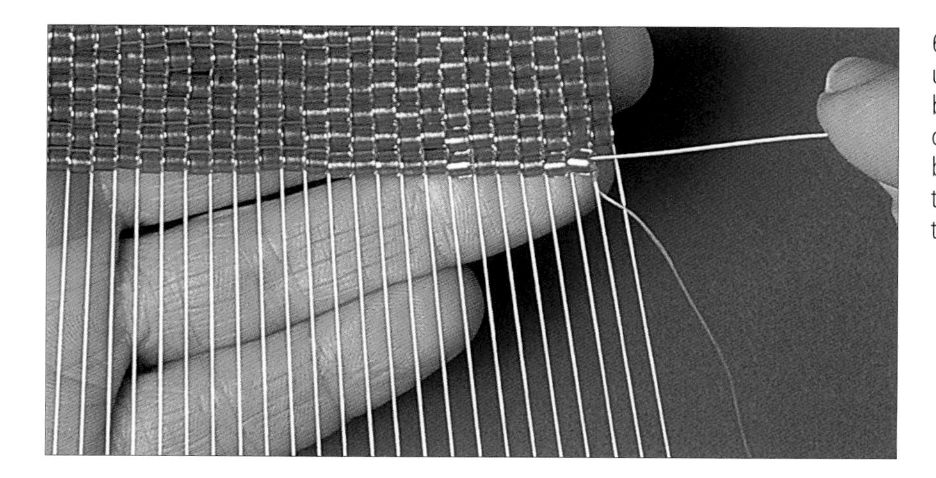

6. Pick up 29 beads, take the weft under the warp and bring it up between the last two warp threads on the right-hand side. Place the beads between the warp threads, then take the needle back across to the left-hand side.

7. Take the thread down between the last two warp threads on the left-hand side. Pick up 28 beads, take the weft under the warp, bringing it up between the second and third warp threads at the right-hand side. Position the beads between the warp threads, then take the needle back across to the left-hand side.

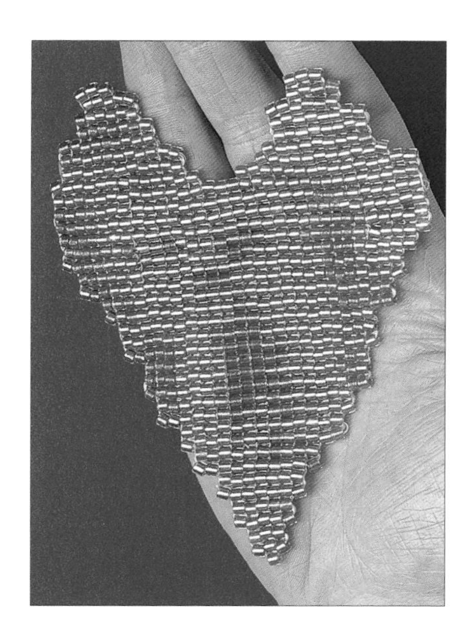

8. Referring to the pattern, continue to weave ever decreasing rows until you reach a row of only one bead. Secure the thread by feeding it into the beads in the row above. Pull it tight and snip off the excess. Turn the loom round and add two small triangles to form the top of the heart using the technique described in steps 4–7. Switch sides on the loom and work an identical heart using purple beads. When both hearts are complete, cut them from the loom and finish off (see page 28) by working all the loose threads back into the beading.

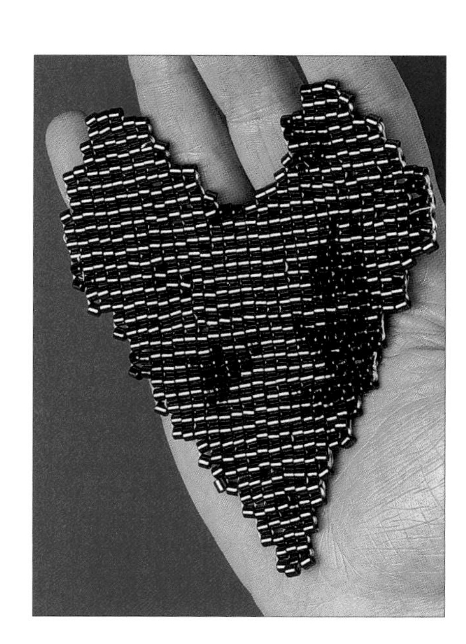

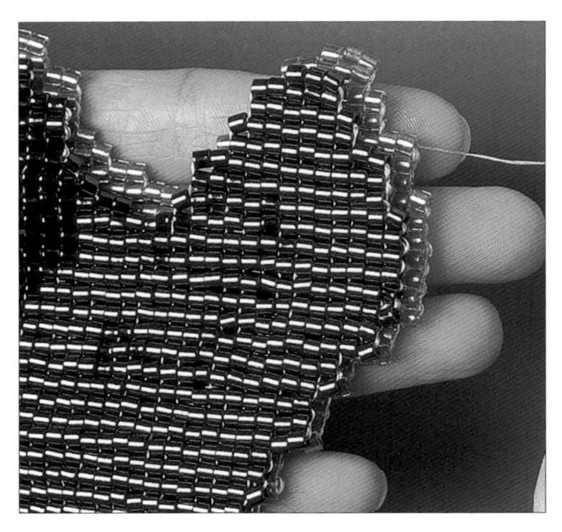

10. The two hearts now need to be joined together. Weave a new length of thread into the pink heart and bring it out at the point shown here. Then place the purple panel on top of the pink.

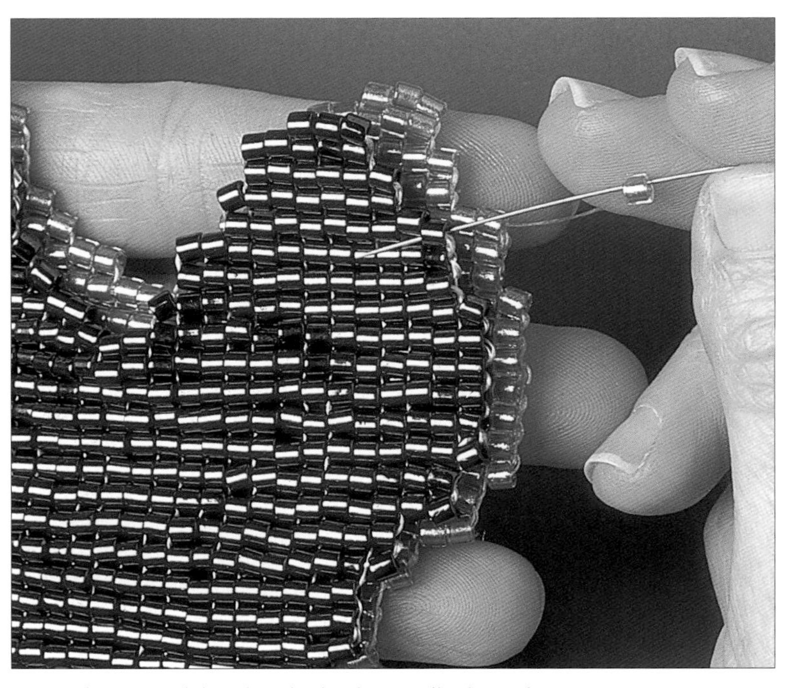

11. Pick up a pink bead and take the needle through the corresponding bead on the purple panel.

12. Pull all the thread through, then take the needle down and through the end bead (purple) in the next row down.

13. Pick up another pink bead and take the needle through the bead directly opposite on the pink panel.

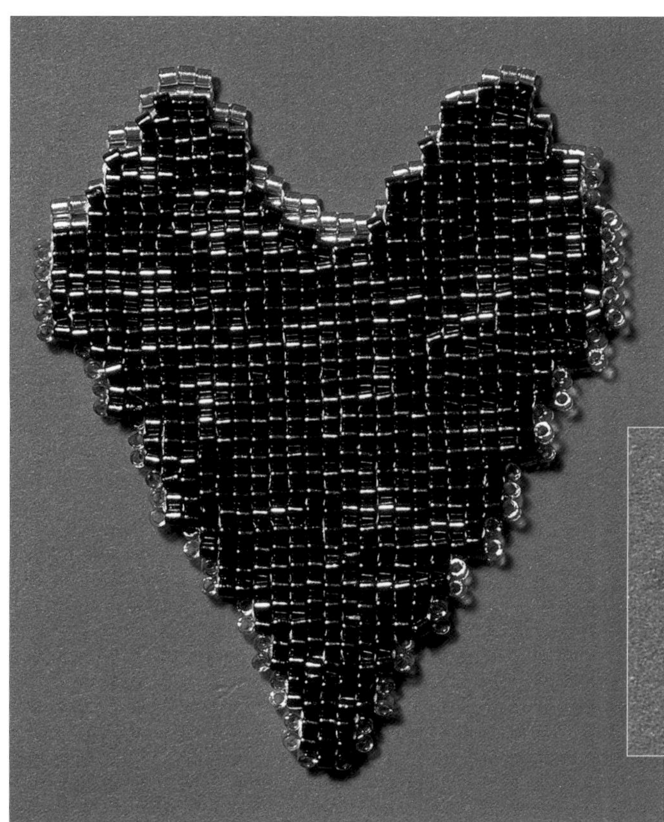

14. Pull the thread through, then take it down and back through the end bead of the row beneath. Work round the shape adding connecting beads until you are level with the start point shown in step 10. To overcome the 'step' between one row of decreased beads and the next, take the needle back into the beading by two or three beads then back out at the end bead of the row below.

15. Now start to work the right-angle weave for the strap. Weave in a new length of nymo and bring it out at the first connecting bead. Pick up three silver beads, then take the needle round and back through the connecting bead.

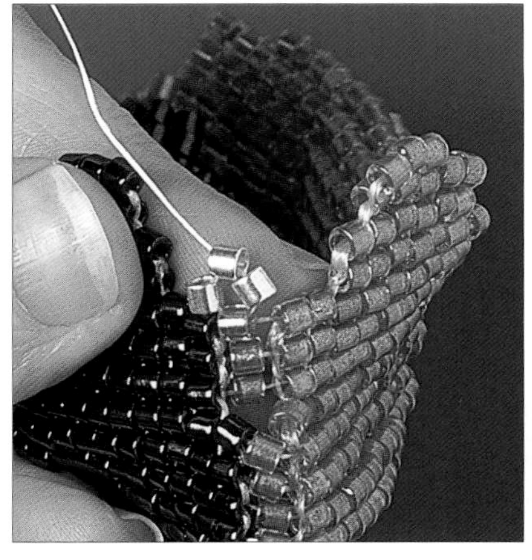

16. Pull the thread through so that the new beads form a loop, then take the needle anti-clockwise round through two of the silver beads to form a loop.

17. Pick up another three silver beads, then take the needle round and back through the top bead in the first loop you formed.

18. Pull the thread through, then take the needle clockwise round through two beads to form a second loop. Pick up another three silver beads and feed the needle through the top bead in your second loop.

19. When you add your third loop take the needle anti-clockwise through two beads. Remember to alternate between clockwise and anti-clockwise in this way as you continue to add loops.

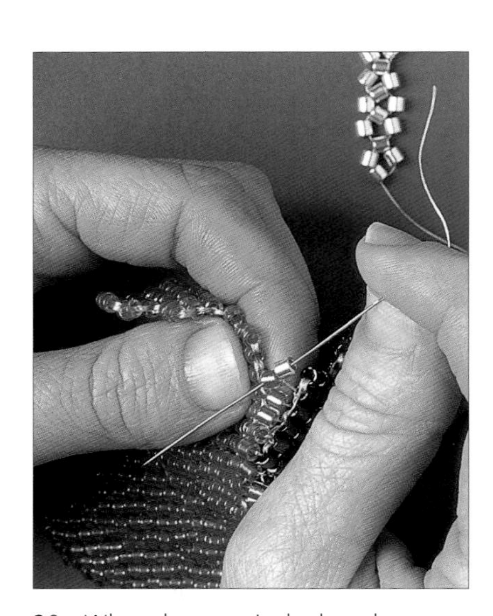

20. When the strap is the length you desire, pick up a silver bead and take the needle through the top connecting bead (right to left) on the other side of the bag.

21. Pull the needle through and pick up another silver bead. Then push the needle left to right through the bottom bead on the last loop of the strap.

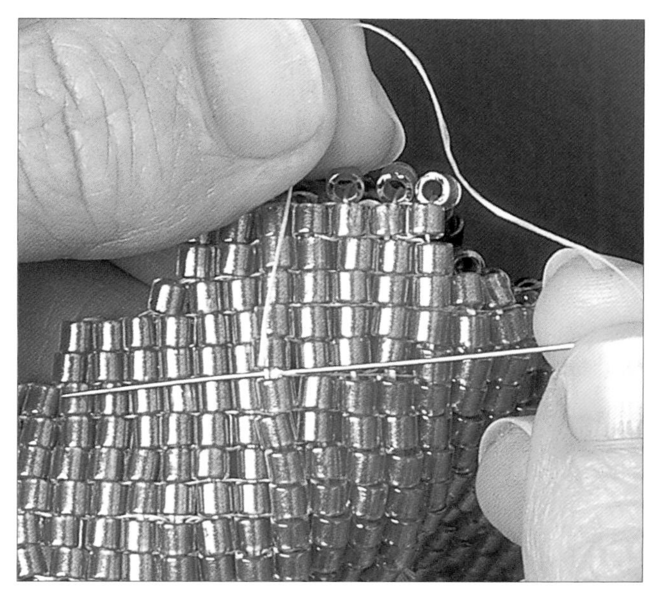

22. Pull the thread tight, then take the needle back through the first of the two silver beads you have just added and then through the pink connecting bead beneath. Push the needle back through several beads on the pink panel and bring the thread up to the top surface. Now take the needle under the weft thread and bring it up between two beads.

23. Pull the thread through leaving a loop and take the needle through the loop. Pull the thread tight to close the knot, weave the thread back into the panel and trim off the excess thread.

24. The strap should now be firmly attached to the bag on one side. Repeat steps 20–23 to attach the strap on the other side.

The beaded hearts that form each side of this bag could be used separately as coasters for a special Valentine's night dinner.

This beaded kimono would look great in a box frame, hung up on the wall.

Dazzling Bag

I have a weakness for Austrian crystal beads and the sparkly fringe on this bag makes the most of their light-catching beauty. I particularly like the combination of sparkling crystals and pretty threads. The ice whites and glittering crystals of this dainty bag make it perfect for a bride but you could also experiment with different colours.

You will need

Large 41cm (16¼in) double-sided upright loom

15 variegated textured threads, 50cm (19¾in)

Nymo, white

Loom beading needle, size 12

Beading needle, size 10

Beads for the bag, fringe and handle, a mixture of seed beads LBC 533 and LBC 334 size 8, 110g

Crystals for the fringe:

- Round AB (4x10mm/7x8mm)
- Cube AB (2x8mm/6x6mm)
- Flat AB (10x8mm/2x6mm)
- Bicone (12x6mm)
- Squashed
  - AB white and alabaster mixed (14x8mm)
  - AB white alabaster (3x6mm)

Crystals for the handle:

- Round (14x8mm)
- Squashed (28x8mm)
- Bicone (16x6mm)

Side-cutters

Memory wire, 9cm diameter (3½in)

Round-nosed pliers

Flat-nosed pliers

Eyepin

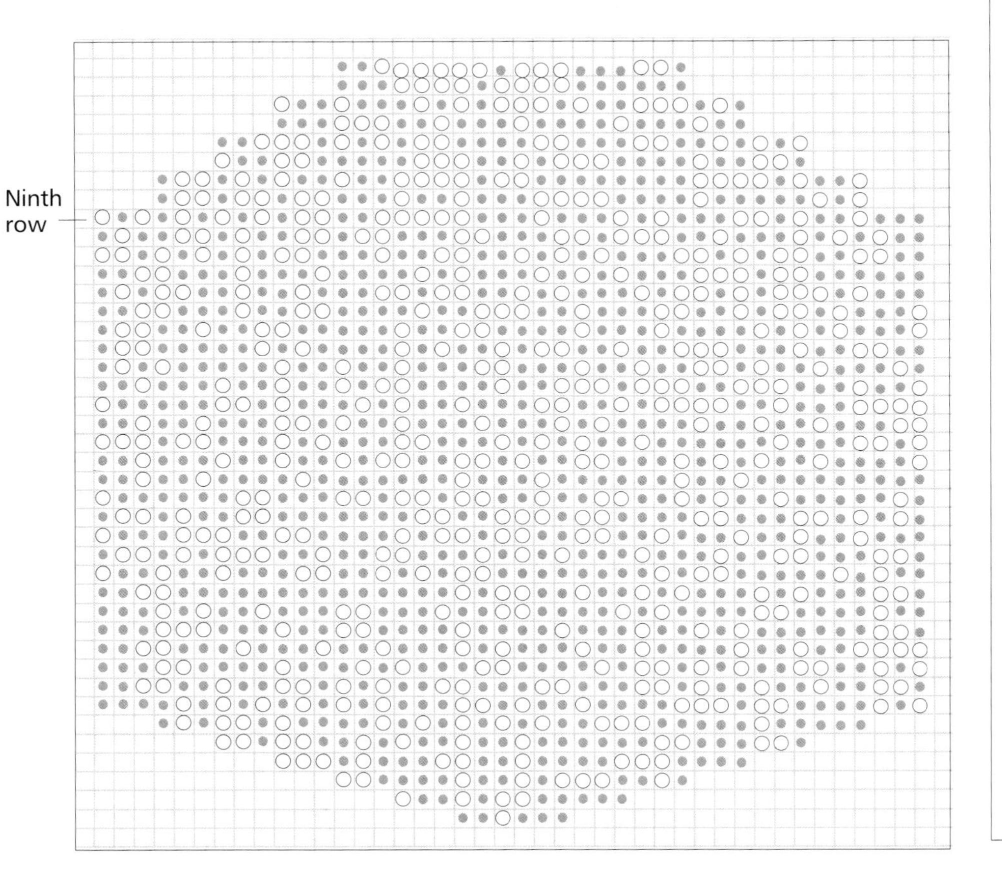

○ • Each patterned square represents a bead but the pattern is random.

Size: 9 x 38cm (3½ x 15in)

The bag has 41 rows of differing lengths. Follow the pattern, and the list opposite, as you decrease the beads.

From the ninth row down:

27 rows 42 beads
1 row 36 beads
1 row 30 beads
1 row 24 beads
1 row 18 beads
1 row 12 beads
1 row 6 beads

From the ninth row up:

2 rows 36 beads
2 rows 30 beads
2 rows 24 beads
2 rows 18 beads

1. Tie the 15 lengths of warp thread to the loom. Following the pattern opposite, work the front panel of the bag starting from the ninth row and positioning it approximately 13cm (5in) down from the separators. Set three seed beads between each warp thread. From the thirty-sixth row onwards, decrease by six beads with each row. When you have beaded to the bottom of the bag, turn the loom around and referring to the pattern, add eight rows to the top. Switch sides on the loom and bead the back panel of the bag. Place the two panels on top of each other, then tie the warp threads from the back and front panels together along the bottom of the bag. Trim the warp ends in a straight line, approximately 14cm (5½in) below the bottom of the bag. Now tie together the front and back warp threads on each corner at the top of the bag. Then make an overhand knot in each individual warp along the top.

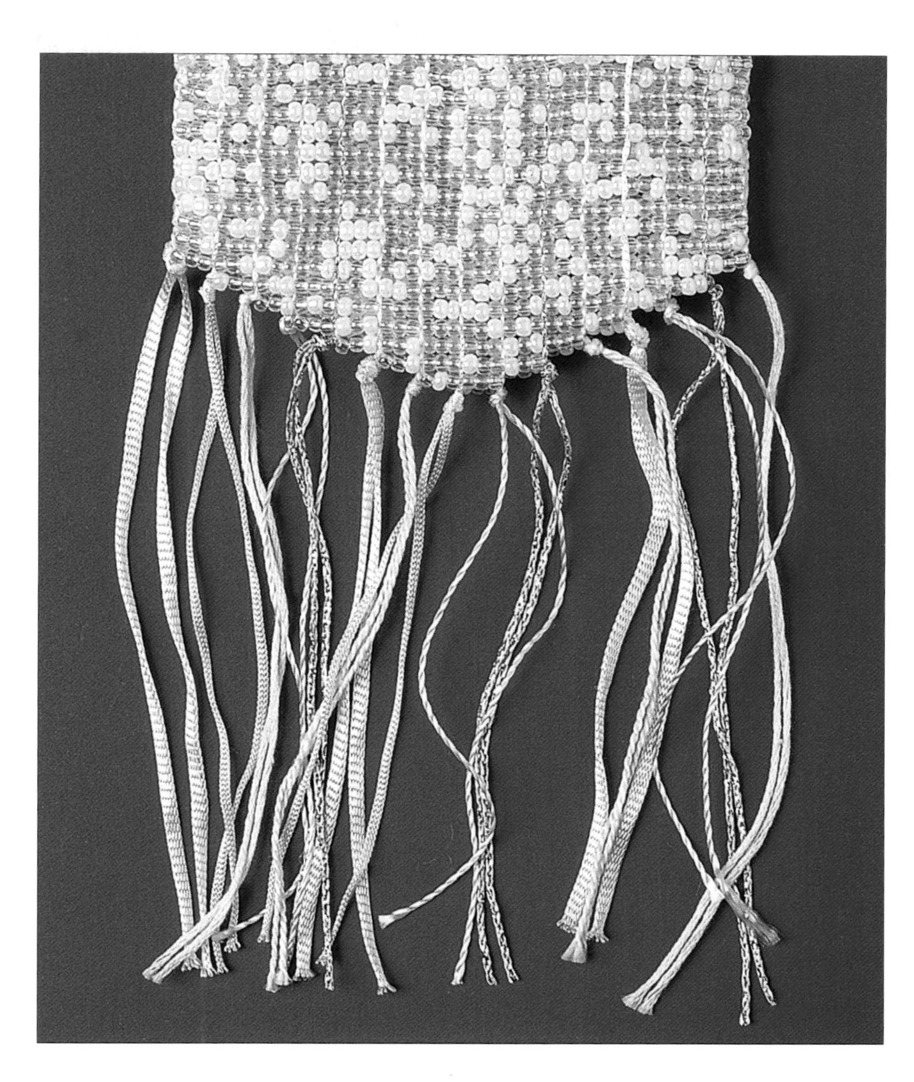

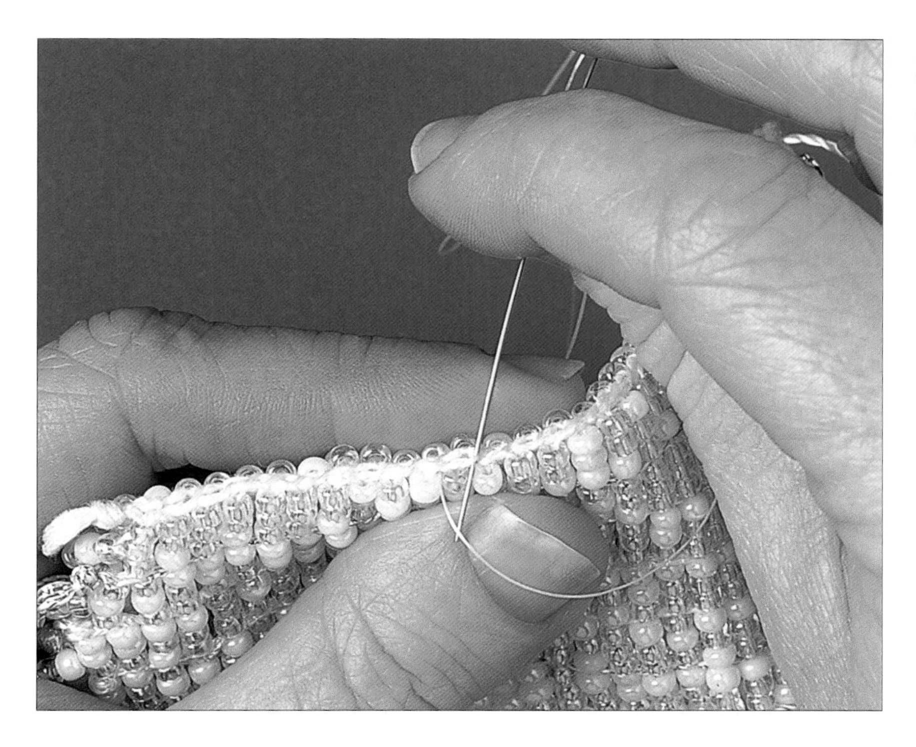

2. Using nymo, sew the sides of the two panels together. Work from the top downwards, sewing through the outer warp threads. Then, oversew all the way back the other way.

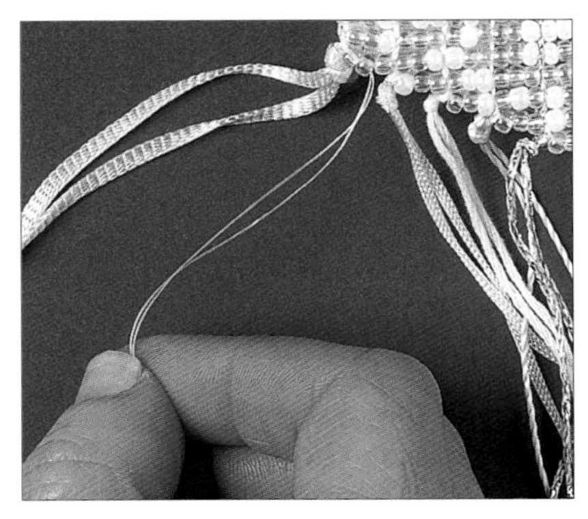

3. To begin adding beaded fringes to the bottom of the bag, first thread the needle with a double thickness of nymo. Weave it into the top panel and exit through the middle bead between the first pair of warp threads.

4. Referring to the pattern below, thread on beads and crystals. At the end of the fringe, bring the needle round the bottom bead and then back up through all the other fringe beads. Feed it back through the middle bead between the first pair of warp threads and then sideways through the adjacent two beads in the panel on the right.

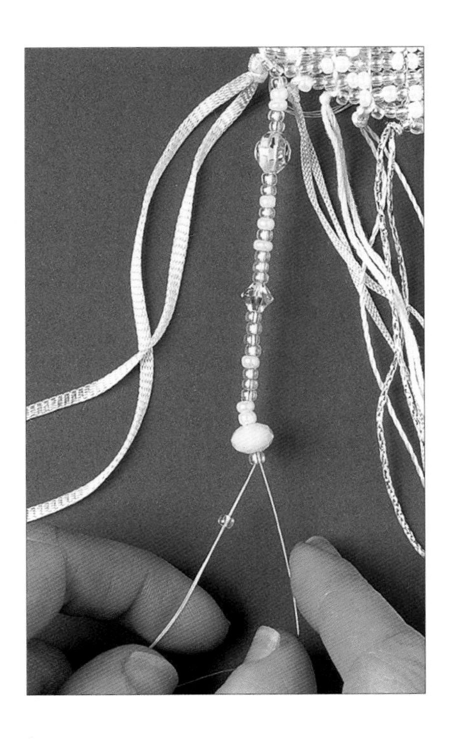

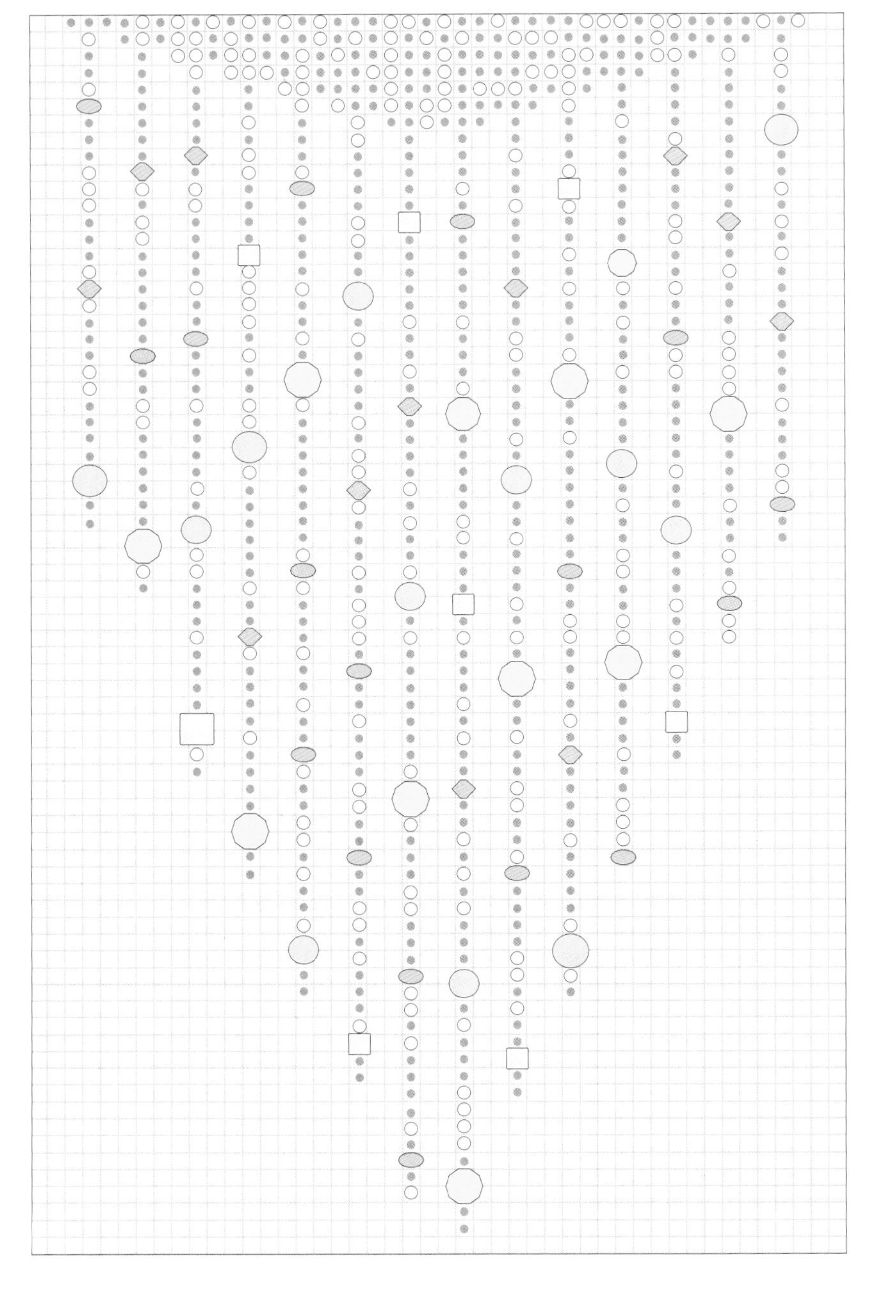

- Squashed opaque (two sizes)
- Seed bead
- Seed bead
- Round faceted
- Bicone
- Squashed
- Flat
- Cube (two sizes)

Use this colour key as you add the crystal fringe.

5. Bring the needle down through the middle bead between the second pair of warp threads. Bead this thread referring to the pattern opposite as before.

6. Repeating steps 3–5, work across the bag adding a beaded fringe to the middle bead between each pair of warp threads.

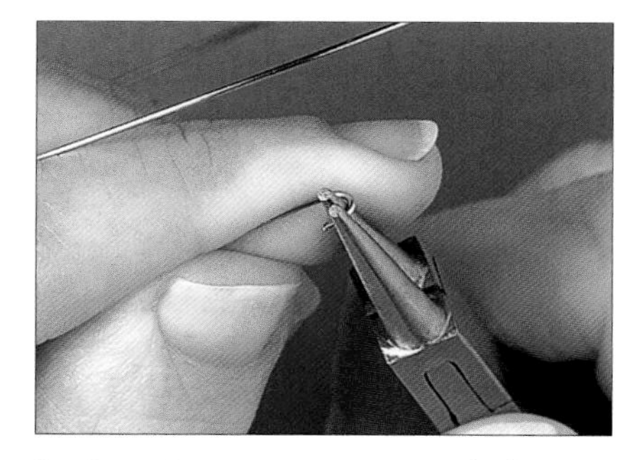

7. Use wire cutters to cut a coil of memory wire with a 6cm (2¼in) overlap. With round-nosed pliers make a loop in one end of the memory wire.

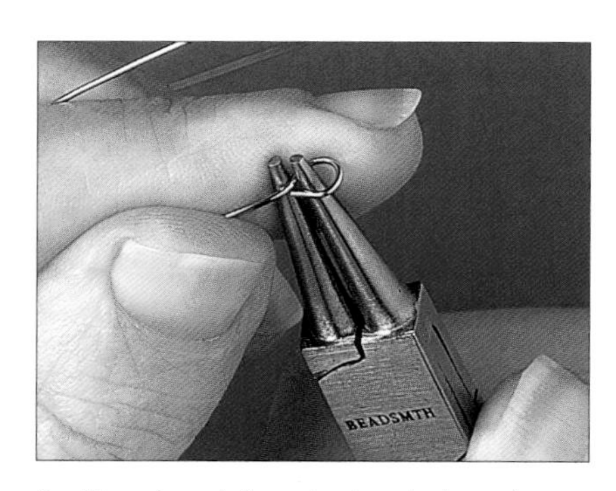

8. Now bend the wire just below the loop to centre the loop on the wire.

9. Thread on an 8mm squashed crystal, a seed bead, a 6mm bicone crystal, a seed bead, an 8mm squashed crystal, a seed bead, an 8mm round crystal and a seed bead. Repeat this pattern two more times, then add another 8mm squash crystal, a seed bead, a 6mm bicone crystal and a seed bead. These form one half of the beaded handle.

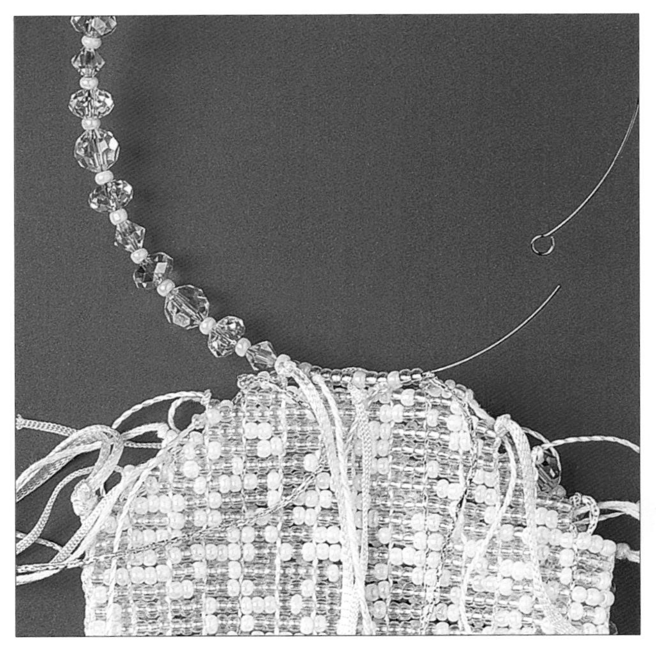

10. Missing out the first and last three beads in the row, thread the memory wire through the beads along the top of the front panel of the bag.

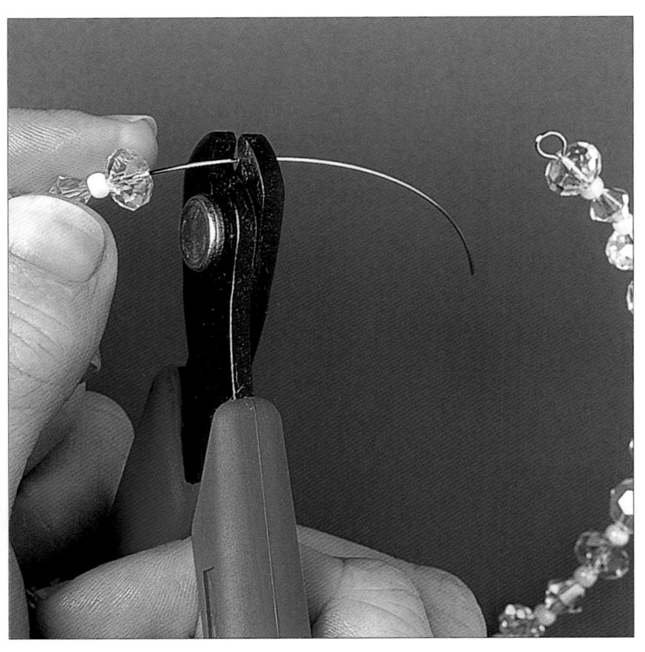

11. Reversing the pattern given in step 9, thread beads on the other side of the handle. Then cut the wire 1cm (3/8in) away from the last bead. Referring to steps 7–8, form another loop on this end of the wire.

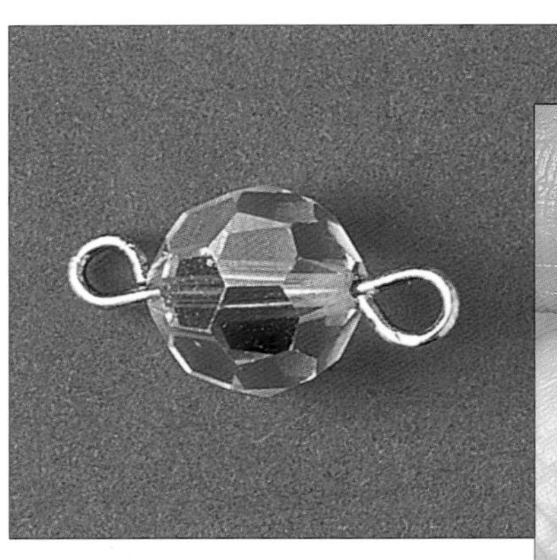

12. Thread a 8mm round crystal on to an eyepin. Trim the end of the eyepin to leave 1cm (3/8in) protruding from the crystal. Form a loop, referring to steps 7–8, to complete the connector piece.

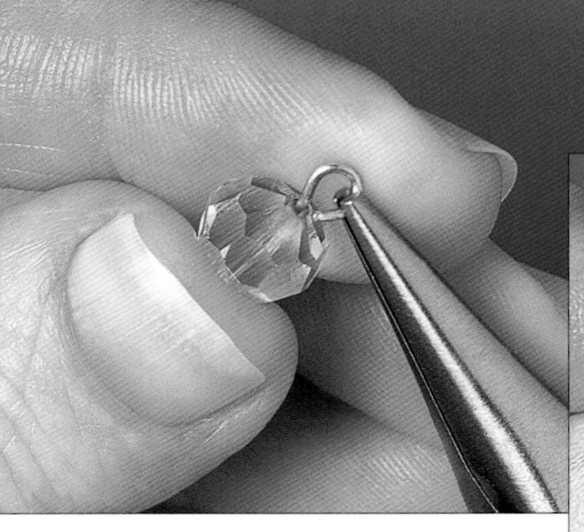

13. Use flat-nosed pliers to bend open one of the connector piece loops.

14. Link the connector piece to the loop on one end of the memory wire, then close the loop. Do the same on the other side of the connector piece. Now repeat steps 7–14 to make and assemble the other handle.

Opposite
This fabulous bag will make you the envy of other party-goers whether you are dressing up a plain outfit or arriving in a gown and tiara.

This candy-coloured purse is the perfect present for a little princess – or a grown-up one!

Opposite
Turquoise beads and coloured threads give this purse a North American Indian feel. It looks great with jeans.

Funky Bag

Most of the projects in this book are based on solid panels of beadwork but do not feel restricted to panels – there are no rules! In this final project I have experimented with leaving large areas of the warp unbeaded. Rows of delicas between the warp threads support the larger crow beads and then the beading is attached to a backing.

You will need

- Large 41cm (16¼in) double-sided upright loom
- Nymo, green
- Beading needle, size 10
- Long darning needle
- Beads:
  - Delicas lime matt AB, 860 x 10g
  - Glass crow beads, clear, 203
- 30 lengths of rattail cord, lime green, 80cm (31½in)
- Mohair yarn, 2 ply, lime green 5m (16¼ft)
- Non-fraying backing material, 23x30cm (9x12in)
- Scissors
- Bag handle, 17cm (6¾in) across

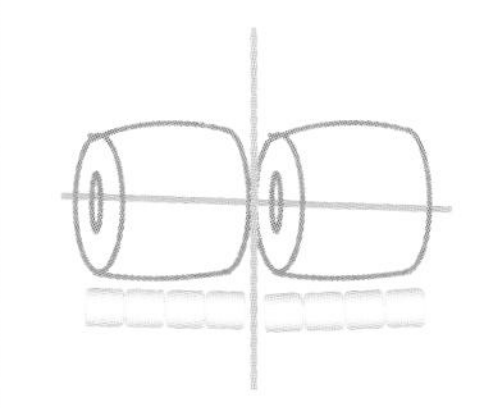

Overall size: 22 x 29cm (8¾ x 11½in)

Green lines represent warp threads. There are four delicas supporting each crow bead between each warp.

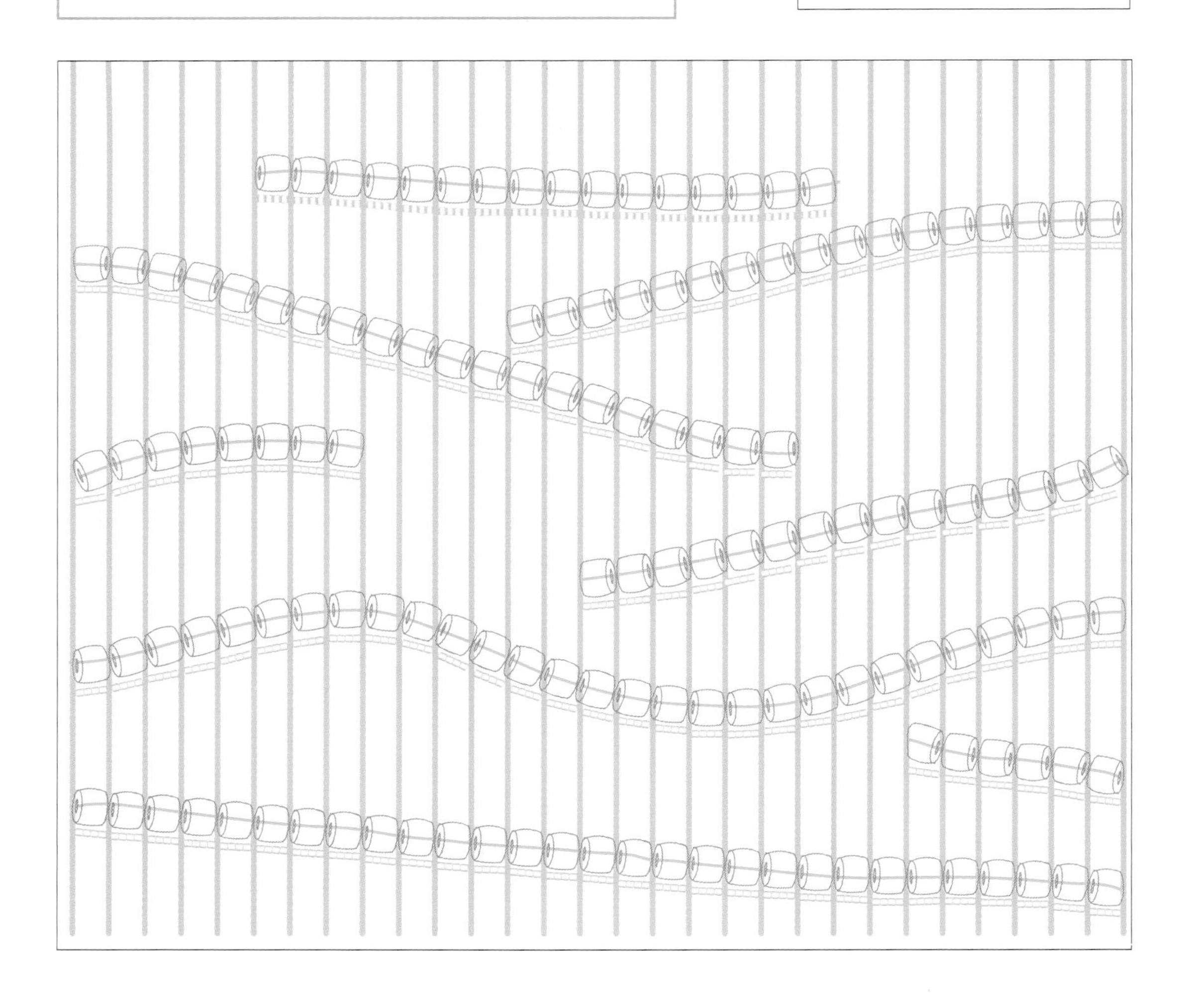

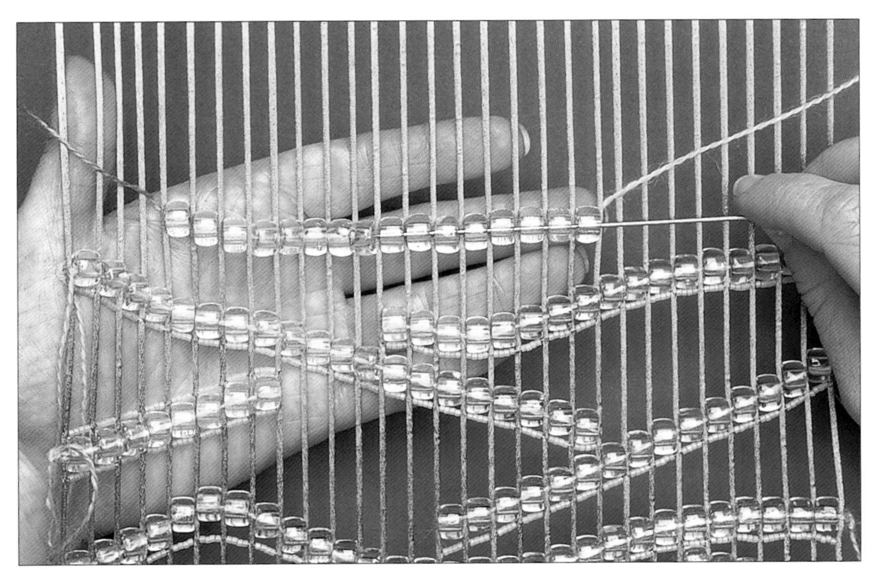

1. Warp up with the 30 lengths of rattail cord. The following steps show the last row in the pattern being added to the design but they apply to all the other rows. Thread the beading needle with mohair yarn and then pick up 16 crow beads. Feed the needle under the warp and position the beads between the warp cords, leaving a loose tail at each end. Now re-thread your needle with mohair yarn and pass it through the middle of all the beads making sure that it goes over, not under, the warp cords. Leave long, loose tails as before.

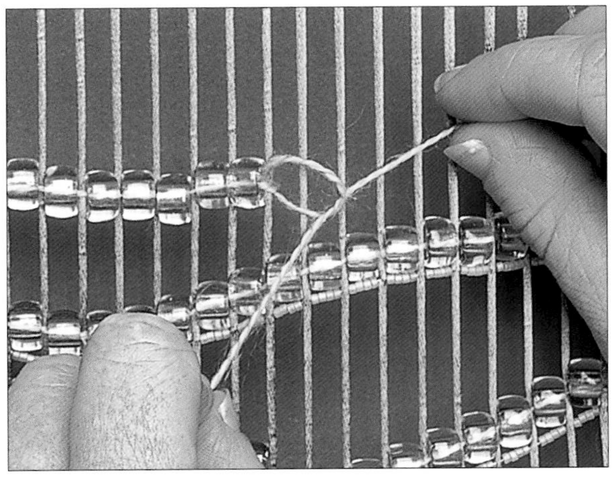

2. Tie double knots at each end of the row, do not make them too tight as you will need to slide them down the warp cord later on. When beading shorter rows, you could use one length of mohair, bringing it round the final warp in the row and back through the crow beads.

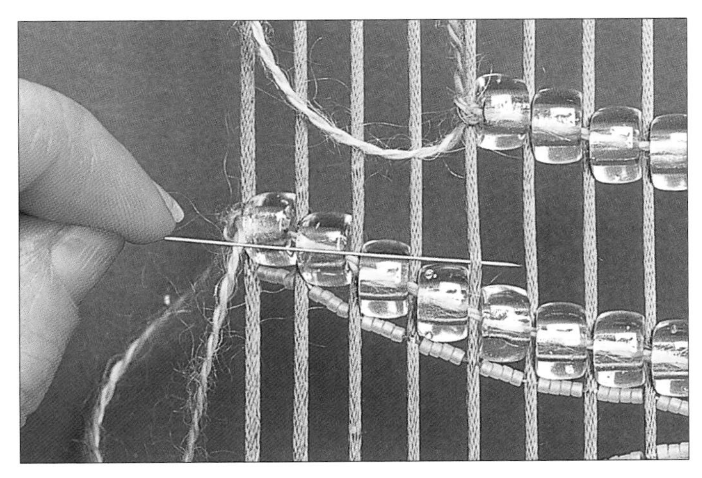

3. Now thread the needle with nymo and secure it to the fifth warp at the point where you want the row to start.

4. Pick up sufficient delicas for the row. Pass the needle under the warp and position four delicas between each pair of warp cords. Push the needle through the final warp cord at the point where you want the row to end.

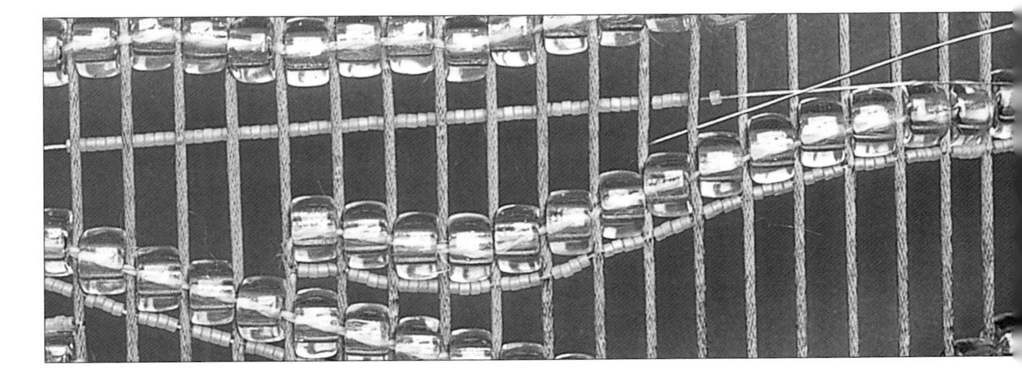

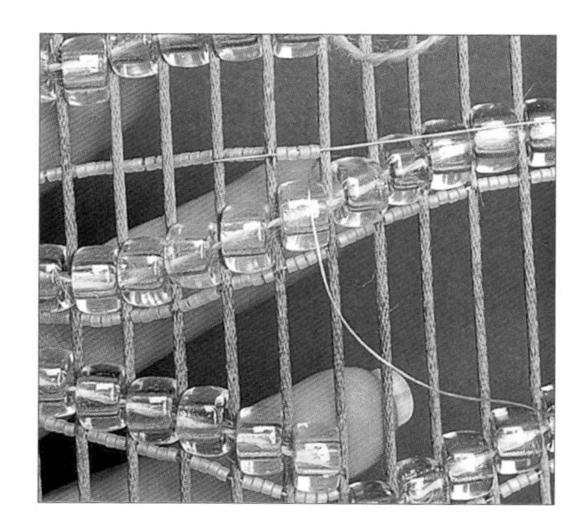

5. Push the needle through the centre of each bead and through each warp cord. It will help if you lift up the beads so that the holes are level with the warp. Adjust the angle of your row as you go to correspond with the pattern.

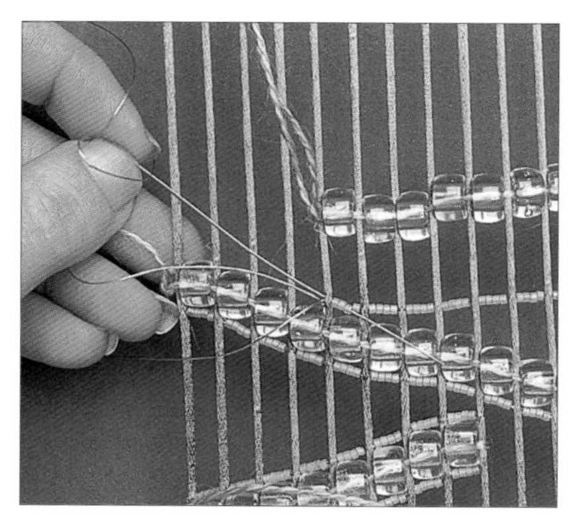

6. When you have completed the row, tie a double knot and push the needle back through three or four of the beads. Snip off any excess nymo.

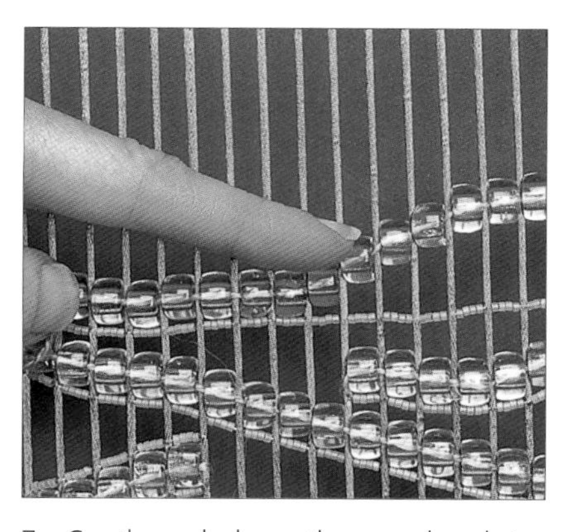

7. Gently push down the crow beads to meet the finished row of delicas.

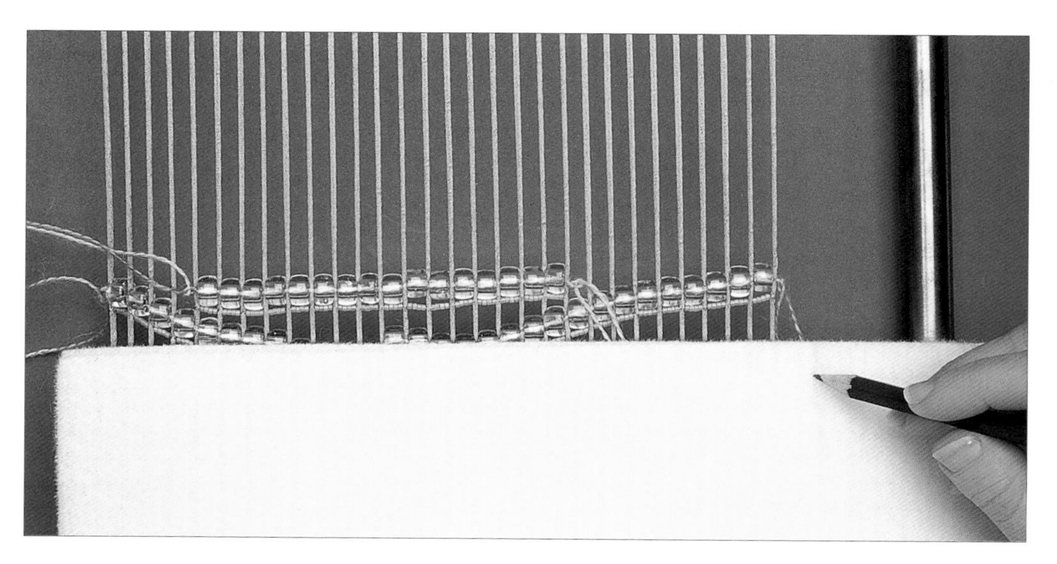

8. The backing can be any non-fraying material. I have used a piece of foam usually used for making beading mats. Fold it in two and measure it against your loom before cutting. Allow 1.5cm (½in) extra at the bottom and top.

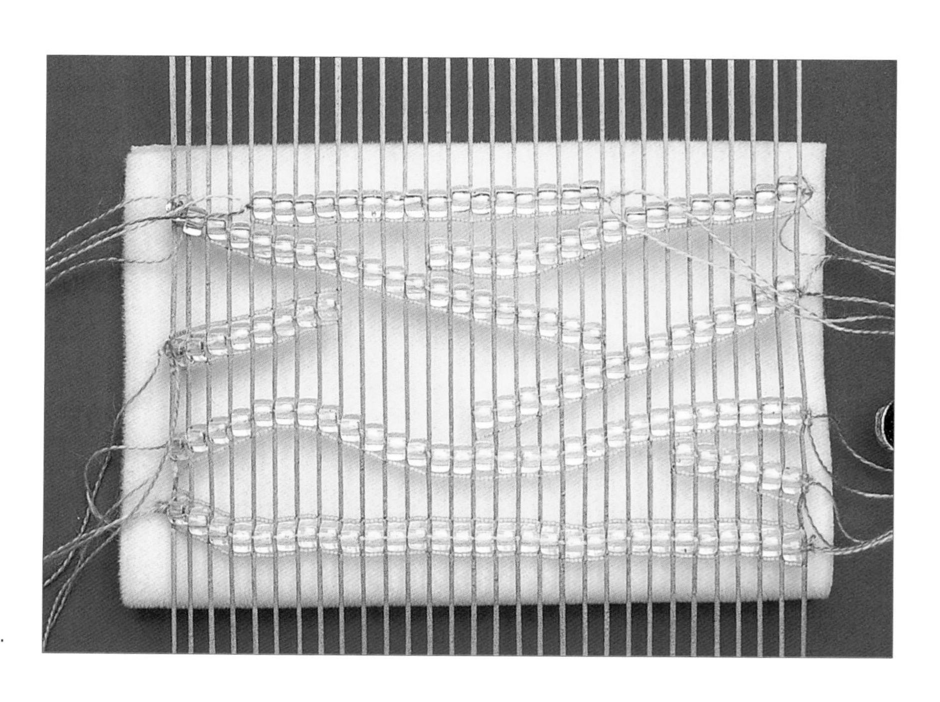

9. Cut the backing to size.

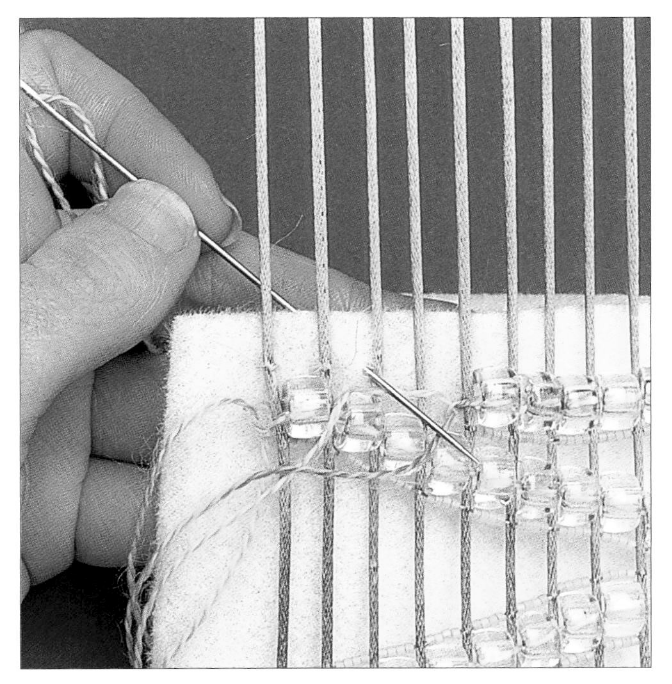

10. Thread the darning needle with mohair and make a little stitch on the back of one layer of the backing. Only sew through the top layer of the backing – do not stitch the tops of the bag together! Bring the needle up through the backing to the left of each warp cord.

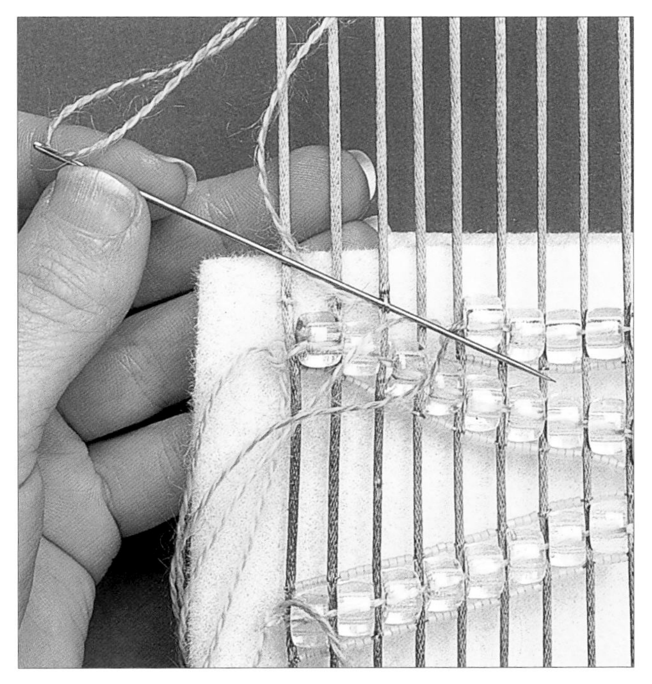

11. Skim the top of the warp cord and push the needle back down through the backing to the right of the warp cord. Finish the row and oversew to secure.

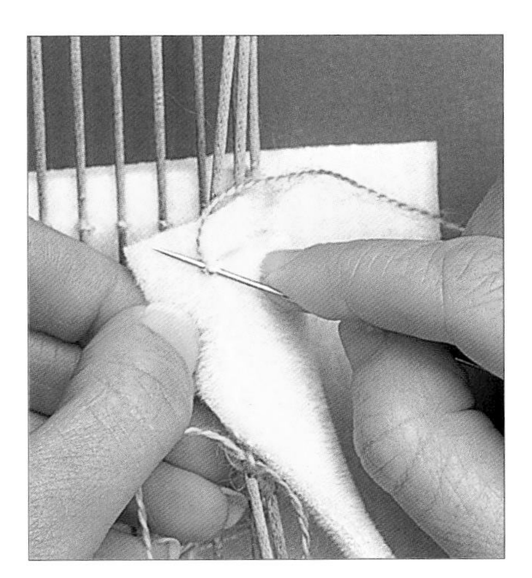

12. Thread your needle with a new length of mohair yarn and secure to the top layer of the backing fabric.

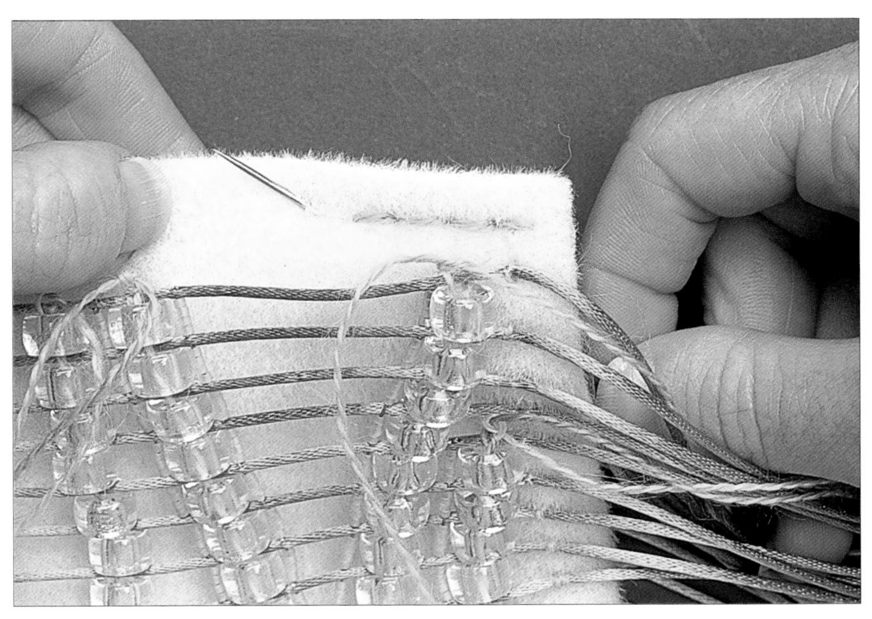

13. Now backstitch along one side of the bag to join the two layers together. With each new stitch, bring the needle up close to the end of the last stitch.

14. Then push the needle back through the base of the last stitch.

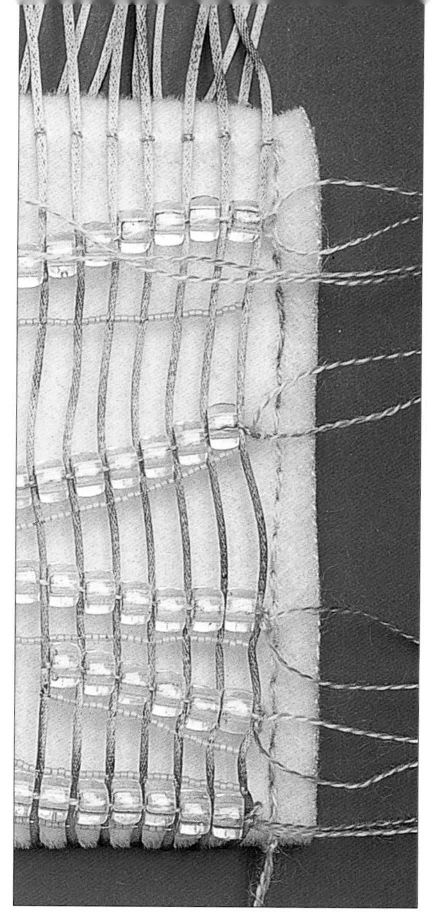

15. Tie an overhand knot at the end of your stitching. Now sew the other side of the bag together in the same way.

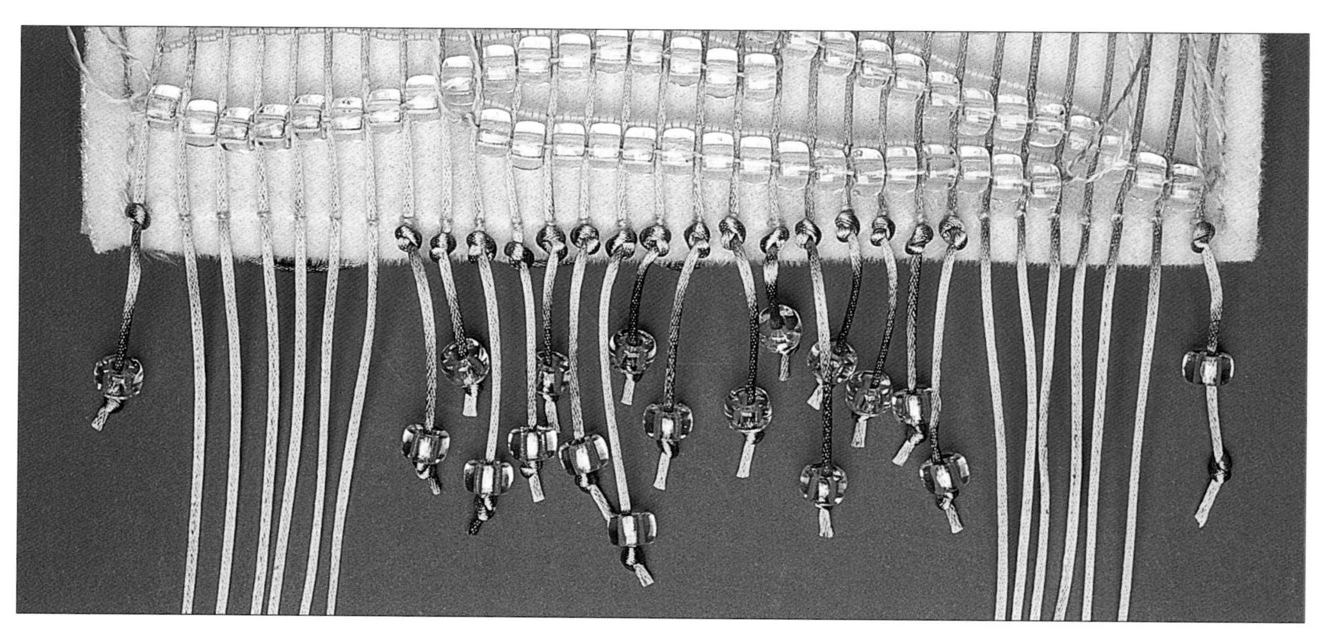

16. Now that the shape of the bag is complete, you can finish off the loose warp cords along the top. Put a crow bead on to the first cord and tie a knot approximately 3–6cm (1–2in) from the top of the bag. Skip 6 cords (these will be used to attach the handle) then bead and knot the next 16 cords, varying the lengths as you go. Skip another 6 threads then bead and knot the final cord. Trim off the ends.

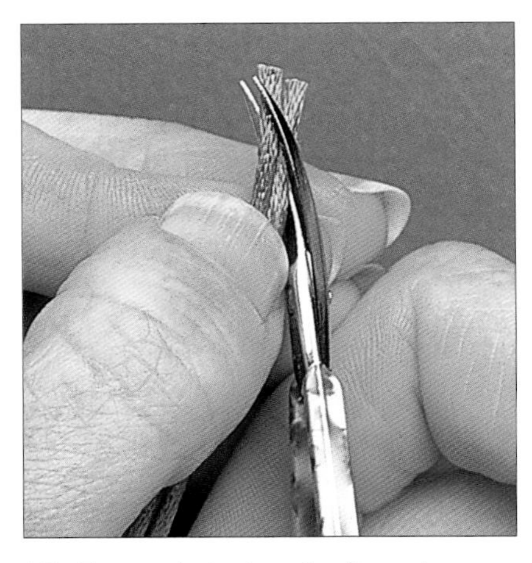

17. To attach the handle, first take two of the six unbeaded cords, hold them together and cut them both on a slant with one snip.

18. Put two crow beads on the pair of cords. Bring the threads through the hole in the handle from the back. Then feed both threads back through the two beads.

19. Repeat steps 17–18 with all the remaining handle cords. Adjust the cords on both sides of the bag until the handles are level, then knot each pair.

20. Add a bead to each pair of cords and knot at the desired length. Trim the ends.

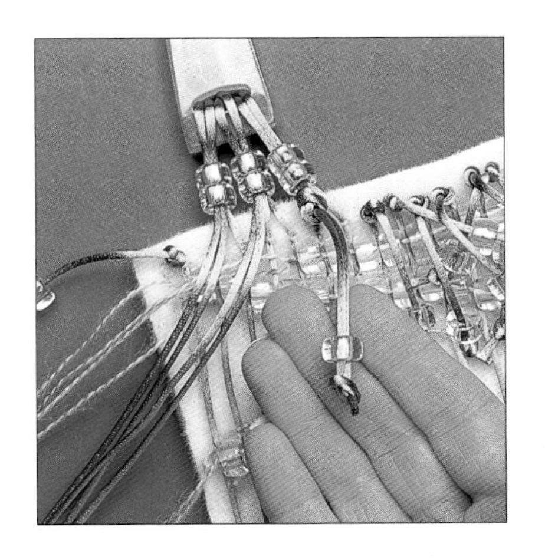

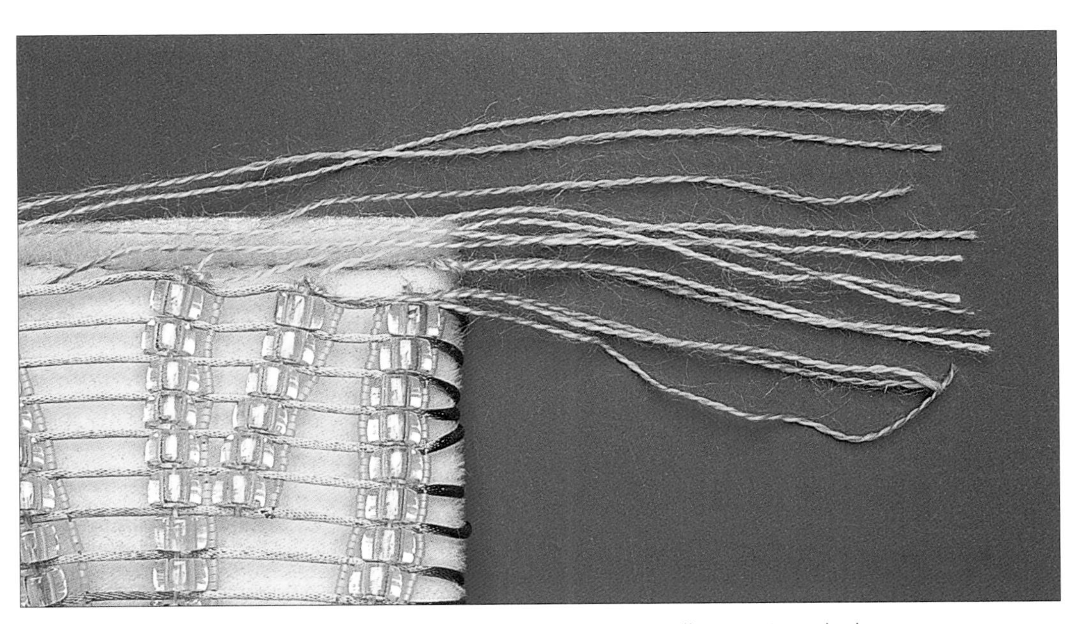

21. Finally, trim the ends off the mohair threads so that they are all approximately the same length. Do not trim too close to the bag, you want them long and loose!

This bag is wonderfully summery and makes me think of sun-dappled lawns.

Opposite

I love this wild design for a bag! I used thick embroidery cotton as the warp and silk ribbon as the weft in this beadwork. Then I attached it to a cone of felt and a bamboo hoop.

Index

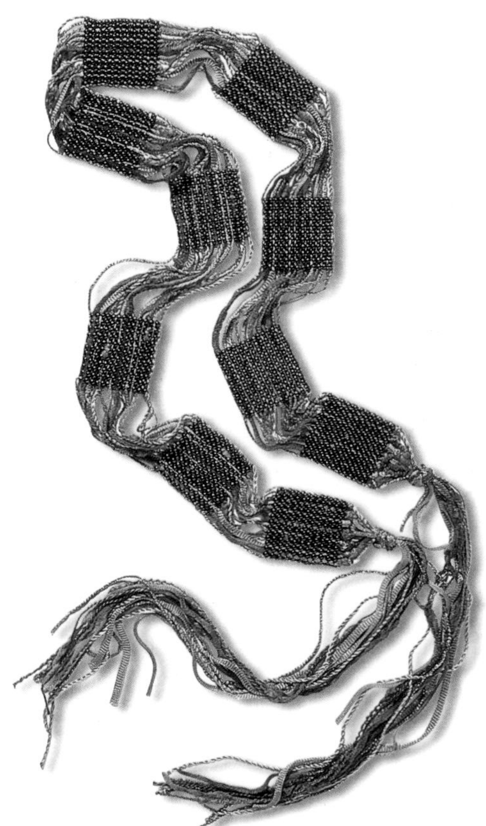